HONESTY
IN THE
CHURCH

by Daniel Callahan

HONESTY IN THE CHURCH

THE MIND OF
THE CATHOLIC LAYMAN

Daniel Callahan

HONESTY
IN THE
CHURCH

CHARLES SCRIBNER'S SONS, NEW YORK

FOR SIDNEY

Contents

Foreword

Every man carries within himself the whole condition of humanity. Within us, in our own breast, where nothing is forbidden and everything is hid, to be honest there—that's the rub!

—*Montaigne*

In an age of overpowering propaganda and hypocrisy the category of honesty demands re-examination. Such a re-examination has been a significant characteristic of the intellectual and cultural history of the contemporary world. On all sides flags for sincerity, integrity and authenticity are unfurled. It would be difficult to determine with any precision just when this passion for honesty, as we know it today, began. For purposes of convenience one might date it from Wordsworth's Preface to the *Lyrical Ballads* in which the poet called for an end to the deceits and artificiality literature had fallen heir to. He set his imagination to the task of reconstructing man's moral being in terms of common language and honestly felt emotions. The Romantic movement, both on the continent and in England, was a serious if often misguided effort to have done with humbug and pretense. Kierkegaard was a fine flowering of that effort.

We are more immediately indebted to the Victorian quest for an ethics of honesty. The best talent of that long and paradoxical era seems clearly to have worshipped at the temple of sincerity. The emphasis was on realism—the world of honest fact and thought. Style, Ruskin thought, was the only morality. But style was the man as well and grew out of a considered awareness of the kind of world we are living in, a deep appreciation of individual worth and a patient curiosity in investigating the possibilities of moral growth. One has only to recall, by way of example, Arnold's great war against Philistinism and Newman's vigorous defense of his intellectual honesty. This, too, was the age of Marx, Darwin and the early Freud—each of whom was responsible for major disclosures of meaning and truth.

We are heirs of that age in at least three ways: in our concern for political structures that would guarantee an expansive morality; in our concern for scientific fact; and, finally, in our concern for emotional honesty as witnessed in some aspects of existentialist and personalist thought as well as in various epistemological considerations. I believe that the fundamental revolution of our time is at bottom a moral revolution and the cornerstone of the new edifice that hopefully will be erected is honesty. That we are far from anything like final success in this enterprise goes without saying. But that there is widespread agreement as to what we are about can scarcely be denied. It is likely that this effort will gather head despite multiple obstacles.

Religion has necessarily been affected by the contemporary moral revolution. It, too, is re-examining its pre-suppositions and goals. Consequently our century has produced some excellent religious thought, both critical and positive. The Catholic has contributed to the new pattern of vision. The Ecumenical Council might be cited as an honest example of the Church's attempt to do some much needed house cleaning. Yet the very hesitations and compromises of Vatican II indicate that narrow-mindedness and inflexibility are powerful influences within the Church. There is, in a word, a problem of honesty among us. I am in wholehearted sympathy

with Mr. Callahan's encouraging and timely confrontation of
this problem. It is to be expected that some will find his book
an angry protest, in very bad taste, indeed a scandal. But on
the whole I anticipate a very favorable reception for it. For
he treats in a forthright and explicit manner what has long
been discussed *sotto voce*.

   Honesty, of course, is not a specifically Catholic problem.
It is a human problem. To be honest, as this world goes, is to
be one man picked out of ten thousand. A substantial body
of current writing furnishes eloquent commentary on the
prince of Denmark's remark. I am thinking in particular of
Jean-Paul Sartre. He uses the example of a café waiter to
illustrate one type of bad faith, an example of one who never
quite manages to strike a note of authenticity because he is
playing *at being* a waiter in a café. There is no small part of
Sartre's waiter in all of us. Bad faith would seem to be as
natural to us as breathing. Sartre sees no way out of the dilemma. Honesty is a species of dishonesty. A constant effort
to be sincere to oneself, he writes, is by the same token a
constant effort to dissociate oneself from oneself. We are
doomed *ab initio* to a Sisyphian labor. But the paradoxical
manner in which Sartre argues this thesis is not distinguished
by clarity. Nor can his metaphysical assumptions be accepted
uncritically; indeed, they are not always consistent with his
own position. Yet it must be granted that he succeeds in illus-
trating the many difficulties of being honest. They are part
of the human situation.

   Even so, there are special, one might say additional,
difficulties for the Catholic. It seems to me a matter of honesty to admit as much. The reasons why this is so are complex.
I should like, in a general way, to adduce the following.

   First, a lingering religious imperialism makes the Catholic Church very reluctant to confront the pluralism of the modern world. We live with the memory of a Church that was once the final arbiter of all values whether spiritual or secular, of a Church that played a major role in creating a civilization. We have inherited some of the spirit of Boniface VIII's *Unam Sanctam* and Pius IX's *Syllabus of Errors.* The *Anathema sit!* is still an expression that comes rather readily to our tongues and our closets are filled with the ghosts of conquistadores and grand inquisitors. This imperialism is betrayed in such expressions as "planting the Church in mission lands," "converting the masses," "controlling the people," "infiltrating the modern world" and the like. Consequently, the emphasis is on institutional efficiency rather than prophetic witness or personal formation. This is why the Catholic can often be very tolerant of the deceptions that are taught in the parochial school system or the various trivialities that are systematically enforced by the present seminary system. He has his eyes fixed on a grandiose goal. A military-legal vocabulary and a dominative ethics borrowed in large measure from the stoical tradition serve well such imperialistic designs.

Secondly, an untenable dualism pervades much of the Catholic's thinking. A this world-other world dialectic is operative in such a way that it frequently leaves him caught between the acts. A very strong and still influential tradition of spirituality has preached a veritable contempt of this world. This accounts in part for the inability of the so-called Catholic countries to cope with pressing social problems; indeed, it goes a long way toward explaining why Catholics at large have such an ambiguous, when not openly indifferent or hostile, attitude toward terrestrial values. One would be very hard put to square such a pie in the sky attitude with the tenets of incarnational theology. I am not suggesting, of course, that this negativity has not to a healthy degree been overcome (at least theoretically) or that there is no such thing as a tenable dualism. My point is a *de facto* one: a false spirituality has encouraged us to take this world all too lightly. I once heard a theologian suggest that the Augustinian basis of much Christian theology is due for a critical overhaul. The limits of the present essay prohibit me from going into that large question. But I must confess that the suggestion excited me very much.

Thirdly, and not unrelated to the point I have just made, an artificial supernaturalism often enables the Catholic to avoid honest confrontation with the realities of this world. Vague appeals to the will of God and the mysterious operations of grace can have pernicious effects. There is nothing so blinding as false or superficial mysticism. A good example of what I have in mind was evidenced last fall in the religious liberty debate at Vatican II. Cardinal Ottaviani argued against the proposal by urging the primacy of "supernatural rights" over the "natural right" of freedom of conscience and was quoted by the *New York Times* (September 24) as saying that "we must profess and defend our Catholic faith no matter what the consequences." The bellicose tone of the Cardinal's remarks is rather frightening. Furthermore, just how supernatural rights could militate against freedom of conscience is rather difficult to imagine. The supernatural is a valid theological category. But when it is invoked to destroy natural values or turn our attention from the reality and beauty of a redeemed world or protect a *parti pris* position then it becomes highly artificial indeed.

Finally, self-interest predominates over charity in much Catholic activity. The acquisition of property and political

power has become a desirable goal. It enables the Church to
re-inforce the status quo and block off enriching synergetic
influxes. Gustave Corcao, in an address to the Second World
Congress for the Lay Apostolate (in Rome in 1958) deplored
such self-interest in these words: "The greatest scandal of
the century is to be found in the fact that Catholics are just
like everybody else. What horrifies non-Catholics is the way
Catholics seem to lack any sense of humble pride in face of the
pomp and circumstance of the world, the way they seem so
fascinated by all the usual signs and symbols of prestige and
power and so ready to bow down before them." By insisting
too much on our rights we diminish the force of our redemp-
tive commitment. There is a psuedo-naturalism that is quite
as dangerous as a psuedo-mysticism. Both compromise the
honesty that is required to worship in spirit and in truth.

In the final analysis, honesty is a matter of truth. The
truth, an evangelical counsel reminds us, shall make us free.
A certain sympathy for Pilate's despairing question goes hand
in hand with modern man's increasing awareness that truth
is to an appreciable extent the kingdom of the possible, the
yet-to-be, which must be actualized by man working under
the inspiration of his own best efforts and the promptings
of grace. The body of tradition, of ancient truths, must be
given new life and often reformulated within the context
of the newness and change that surround us. How must the
Catholic relate himself to this situation? In what sense is his
claim "to have the truth" to be interpreted? Is his faith an
"answer" to the modern quest? Is truth a multiple, always
partial achievement? Or is it a final acquisition that can be
stated in objective, perennially valid language? These are the
relevant questions. They are also multi-dimensioned questions.

Nicholas Berdyaev says something pertinent about this matter. "The faith of man," he says, "has to go forward through criticism, through struggles of the spirit; it is only thus that it acquires the highest value. Man moves forward through doubt, through dichotomy, through suffering, and only in the overcoming of them all does he become spiritually tempered and ready for the highest degree of spirituality. That which takes place in man and with man in history has an immense importance for the plenitude of divine-human truth. The world changes in accordance with the standpoint from which it is viewed. Nor is it only the view of the world which changes; the view of what is revealed of the other world, the higher world, changes also."

This mentality is gradually taking root in the Catholic body. The developments of recent decades, while still limited both in their motivations and influences, are impressive evidence that such is the case. Many linchpins of the older structure have yet to be removed. But I am confident that this will be done and yet more effective ones will replace them. I am thus confident because I believe in the possibilities of honesty for which Mr. Callahan so earnestly pleads in this book.

BERNARD MURCHLAND, C.S.C.

CHAPTER ONE

The Claims of Honesty

A BOOK on "honesty in the Church" requires some explanation. After all, one might well say, of course there must be honesty in the Church, but what need is there to devote a book, even a small one, to this truism? Is not the Church in its essence devoted to truth? Is it not the very manifestation and embodiment of truth, the truth of man redeemed, of Christ triumphant, of the Holy Spirit present among the people of God? "This is why I was born, and why I have come into the world, to bear witness to the truth" (John 18:37). Is it not, then, essential that the Christian put falsehood behind him?

Properly speaking, such questions are, or ought to be, just what they seem: rhetorical questions, the answers to which are known the moment one frames and asks them. But even rhetorical questions with obvious answers need, on occasion, to be examined afresh. For it is by no means evident that when the Catholic talks about "truth" he means anything more than the truth of certain theological propositions: that what he affirms as true corresponds with reality in some objective sense. So, too, when he thinks of "honesty" he may be prone to think of it only insofar as it bears on the telling of the truth to others: he knows he must not bear false witness. To be honest, then, would be taken by many to mean: do not say anything which does not correspond with "the facts."

But this does not exhaust the matter—not at all. The main drawback is that such a rough conception of honesty takes little account of the inner person, of that province of man's being which is inaccessible to others. It is in that province— commonly called the "subjective"—where the problem of honesty takes on a different character. "The facts," for instance, about one's real attitudes, dispositions, and beliefs are far harder to uncover than "the facts" about the external world. If someone asserts that he is thirty-nine years old, he should have little difficulty knowing whether he is telling the truth. By contrast, a man may assert that he believes in equal rights for Negroes, yet at the same time have a dim suspicion that in his innermost self he is not nearly as certain of his convictions as he makes himself out to be. Even if he tries very hard he may not be able to determine decisively exactly what he does believe.

It is one thing to be honest with others, and quite another to be honest with oneself. Here is the place where "honesty in the Church" becomes an urgent issue. The Church is at present in the midst of two crises bearing on honesty. The first is whether, in the public sphere, it can be honest about its past and present faults, its need for reform, its unfulfilled promise. This is of consummate importance for the future of ecumenism and Catholic renewal. Can the Church openly admit that its inner life does not measure up to its principles? Can it admit that its principles are not always as irreformable as has sometimes been taught? The second is whether the Church can allow its members to bring out into the open their most secret anxieties, dilemmas, and concerns. Actually, the two crises merge into one. The

Church will be honest in public only if the Catholic is able to be honest in the Church. A Church which cannot be honest with itself can hardly be expected to be honest with others.

I call this a "crisis" deliberately, with no intention of using inflammatory language. The public crisis stems from the fact that, after centuries of proclaiming its purity, the Church does not know how far it can safely admit that it has gone astray, been in error, or failed to live up to its divine mandate. Here and there various Catholic writers, theologians, bishops—and even popes—have admitted that the Church is not always what it should be or claims to be. But the language of such admissions is customarily vague. It is rare to find a pope or a bishop pointing his finger at some specific failure on the part of the Church. This is not surprising, for any suspicion that the Church may be, in actuality, something other than spotless is bound to be unsettling for many. This will be particularly true of those raised and educated to believe that the Church's special claim to allegiance rests on its purity of doctrine, life, and practice. Any suggestion that the Church can make mistakes—may *now* be making mistakes—is an immediate threat to the psychological security of many. It is not just a threat to the ordinary faithful. It may be just as strong a danger to the professional theologian. He too may have a heavy stake in the certainty that the Church can do no wrong. Even those perfectly willing to concede that the Inquisition, for example, was wrong if not wicked, may find themselves far more defensive when it comes to the actions of the Church in the twentieth century. To find fault with a Renaissance pope is perfectly acceptable today; to find fault with Pius XII, John XXIII, or Paul VI is taken to be disrespectful.

That is part of the present public crisis in the Church.

The private crisis—or better, the crisis of individual Catholics in the Church—is somewhat different, though not unrelated to the public one. Put briefly, the Catholic rarely knows how free he is to express fully his thoughts, his doubts, his perplexities, his hopes within the Church. He does not know the extent to which those in authority will allow him to make known his inner life. Nor does he know how far the Church will allow him even to confront himself. He knows he is free to say safe things, commonly accepted things, but how free is he to voice dangerous opinions? How free is he to think honest, disturbing thoughts even if he does not express them? I am not talking here about expressing "critical" opinions about this or that policy or ecclesiastical decision. The Church is now learning to live with a considerable amount of institutional self-criticism. Instead, I am thinking about the freedom of the individual Catholic to say openly that he finds a particular doctrine unconvincing; to admit that he has serious reservations about central matters of Catholic teaching; to reveal that he finds it impossible, however hard he tries, to fulfill some precept of the Catholic law; or to concede that, in some ultimate personal upheaval, he has doubts about his faith. This, I am convinced, is a painfully real crisis for a considerable number of Catholics today. They often feel they have only two clear choices: to suffer obediently in silent conformity, or to leave the Church. Whether there can be a third, middle way, is, perhaps, the most critical question facing anyone who would attempt to discuss "honesty in the Church."

Secular Roots of the Crisis

It is difficult to understand the present crisis without first observing how the consciousness of modern man is being reshaped by the contemporary world. For my purposes, one element of this change is especially pertinent. That I will call the "rejection of convention." By this I mean that many people, threatened and coerced by powers beyond their direct control, have come to distrust those conventions of society which seem to contribute to their sense of helplessness and nakedness. Moreover, they have come to be suspicious of any ideological abstractions which appear to bolster and sustain them. There are some who might prefer to talk of a rejection of authority rather than of convention. Hardly a day goes by in which some priest, minister, or other civic guardian of virtue does not decry a loss of respect for authority, among youth, students, wayward citizens, or whatever group seems at the moment most out of step with community standards. But I think it more helpful to speak of a rejection of convention. Even the rowdiest, most untrammeled groups seem willing to pledge their loyalty to a new prophet should they find his message pertinent to their needs or desires. What is rejected is any suggestion that a way of life or a belief is valid simply because custom supports it.

The sources of this rejection are manifold. In recent history, Nazism fed on the idea that, regardless of the shortcomings of Hitler and his followers, they represented the government of Germany. Thus it was easy for the German citizen to justify support of the regime: nationalistic conventions, common to the Western world, dictated that a citizen should support his government when the nation is faced with external threats. Even if the government brought these threats on itself by its evil deeds, even if the officials were vicious men, the one thing that counted was the duty of everyone to defend his homeland. Moral niceties, competing views on justice, political rights—all these things could be ignored for the duration of the war. "My country, right or wrong."

One of the lessons of the Eichmann case was that men will commit the most atrocious crimes on the basis of the conventions of the society to which they have given allegiance. The German military convention held that the individual did not have the right, much less the obligation, to pass moral judgment on the orders given him by his superiors. No one with any knowledge of this style of self-justification among the Nazi hierarchy, or among those German citizens who passively watched the Jews transported to their doom, could fail to see the evil inherent in the indiscriminate acceptance of "community standards." Totalitarianism can thrive only where assent to convention is taken as the proper duty of the good citizen. It can thrive only where conformity is accounted a virtue, and where querulous skepticism is accounted a threat to the common good.

Yet in the light of recent history, it is difficult to deny the apparent value of skepticism, a value fully confirmed by the history of Communism. In too many cases, the free world has seen with a searing force that innocent, well-meaning people—especially when they are already docile to convention—can be manipulated and used by corrupt authority. The modern totalitarian government has at its disposal immensely effective tools of coercion and deception. It can lie to the people so effectively that they can barely guess at the truth. It can send men to a meaningless death totally convinced they are dying for a holy cause. It can cover its own tracks so effectively that there is no way for the average person to discover the truth even if he wants to know it. In one sense, then, only the congenital skeptic is safe, only the person who hesitates to believe anything, who doubts on principle all convention, all custom, all authority.

Contemporary man is beginning to notice the danger of

unreflective, traditional responses. If World War II was not
sufficient to bring them to his attention, the danger of a nuclear war is. The prospect, or possibility, of a nuclear disaster
has effected a major revolution in man's thinking, making
clear to him that automatic reactions could touch off such a
war. Both the citizen and the statesman, for instance, now
realize that a slight to a nation's "dignity" is not sufficient
reason to initiate an armed redress even though such a response would have been taken for granted by earlier generations. More important still, the possibility of nuclear war
has made men reflect more deeply on the utter stupidity of so
many wars and incidents. What kind of world do we live in
where our enemies of twenty years ago are now our bosom
allies, and our former allies are now our enemies?

Faced with such apparent absurdities, is it any wonder
that the words "patriotism," "duty," "national honor" fail to
sound with their old resonance? In the last half-century millions of people have been killed because of their bewitch-
ment with these powerful abstractions. Even those who see
that they are not wholly bad cannot help approaching them
with greater wariness. History, in brief, has made a mockery
of man's conventions. They have not been worth the price in
lives and torment necessary to sustain them. They can be
taken for granted no longer.

The wars of the twentieth century have not been the
only sources of disillusionment. Despite the passing of over
one hundred years since the Emancipation Proclamation, the
American Negro still lives a life of partial bondage. Neither
the Bill of Rights nor the Federal Courts have been able fully
to implement the American ideal of equality for all. For the
Negro, the disillusionment has been particularly sharp. But
for many whites as well, dedicated to Negro freedom, the

failure of so much of the nation to take equality seriously has undercut their optimism: frustration, despair, and a sense of all-pervasive stupidity and hard-heartedness have dealt a body blow to faith in convention. For in the end, it is custom and ingrained mores which have sustained segregation and discrimination: in theory, freedom for the Negro; in practice, the maintenance of the status quo. Freedom, yes: as long as the Negro stays in his place.

This discrepancy between professed belief and actual practice, so acute in the racial crisis, has helped to shatter a sustaining faith in the power of convention to guarantee the good life. The discrepancy is also seen in business, where the supposed ideal of free competition actually covers the accepted existence of widespread price-fixing; in publishing, where the idea of a free press is often prostituted to commercial interests; in television, where a fear of the "controversial" is enough to induce advertisers to withdraw sponsorship of a program (even though what is said to be "controversial" may be, and often is, something accepted by millions); in government, both local and national, where politicians who hail the necessity of virtuous leaders themselves turn out to be men who use their office for their own financial gain—or place the interests of their supporters before the common good, or take a position which pleases the press and their backers even though they may know it to be an irresponsible one. Tribute is paid to the pieties of life, but not to the realities.

Hazlitt once wrote: "The only vice that cannot be forgiven is hypocrisy." Contemporary literature abounds in themes which stress this point. Whether a Sinclair Lewis or a Mencken in an earlier generation, or a J. D. Salinger, a Jack Kerouac, a James Baldwin in our own, the abhorrence of hypocrisy has become almost the ultimate single standard about which twentieth-century man can rally. The appeal of this standard is reflected in the way publishers and reviewers will often proclaim a novel's "honesty," the "sincerity" of an author's vision, the "candidness" of an autobiography. In contrast, those who celebrate traditional ways of life can expect to take a critical drubbing: few will be willing to credit them with integrity. Philosophy, too, has seen an emphasis on authenticity, especially in the writings of the existentialists. There is a rejection of elaborate systems, a repudiation of philosophical thought which departs from the concreteness of man's life, a wariness about utopianism. Though empiricists and linguistic analysts have little in common with existentialists, they share a mutual suspicion of abstractions, a common desire to show the mistakes and evasions in traditional ways of philosophizing. If their tone is not as shrill as that of the poets and novelists, if their passions are more restrained, the point is remarkably similar. This is a critical and in many ways a skeptical age. Man's wariness expresses itself in every form of human creativity.

The enemy, again, is convention, and it has spurred a cry for honesty. It is a cry which says: Tear off the masks which men and institutions wear; look under the surface of professed virtue; rip away the rhetoric which covers injustice; bring into the open the reality of self-interest and venality; expose the way leaders operate, the way "God-fearing" men give the lie to the religion they profess to honor. It is a cry which sometimes cannot help exclaiming: Men are frauds; institutions are frauds; life itself is a fraud. It is a cry which springs from a horrible realization that too many grand schemes have proved to be delusions; that too many innocent people have been gulled to lay down their lives for values which turn out to be only empty slogans; that too many rigidly held certainties amount to nothing more than thoughtless conformities. It is a cry based on a recognition that valuable ideas, needed reforms, and genuine possibilities of renewal have been rejected out of hand because they shocked too many people, or threatened vested interests, both material and psychological.

Once one has taken a peek below the covers, and found the world caught up in evil, doubt and distrust seem the sensible point of departure. That is the spirit which is capturing our age, slowly but surely. It is especially the spirit which is capturing the young. They have seen their parents caught up in too many follies, victimized by too many conventions of life and thought, tricked by too many witch doctors and medicine men. They grow up watching their parents deny in practice what they so fervidly proclaim as the standards their children should abide by. They see that hypocrisy can kill the good, not just false values or ideologies.

The Protestant Quest for Honesty

It is a good rule of thumb to assume that when an important mood begins to dominate secular society, it will also make its appearance within the churches. Hence one should not be surprised to discover that a vigorous quest for honesty is now gaining rapid momentum within Protestantism. Its existence was most prominently displayed in the Bishop of Woolwich's book *Honest to God*.[1] In that book Bishop John A. T. Robinson of the Church of England managed to capture brilliantly the mood of many Protestants. Just as Hans

[1] Philadelphia: The Westminster Press, 1963.

Küng, in *The Council, Reform and Reunion*,[2] brought to full consciousness the reform movement in Catholicism, so Bishop Robinson brought to the surface the profound distress that many Protestants feel when they look at the state of their religious convictions and of their churches.

Among the reasons for the Protestant malaise is the widespread conviction that much that has passed for traditional theology no longer has meaning for contemporary man; that the Protestant churches have been displaced from their earlier positions of cultural dominance; and that the ethical and cultural values supported by the churches do not sufficiently meet the demands of our present-day technological society. In concentrating his attention on the present state of theism, on the place of the Christian in the world, and on the traditional conception of Christian ethics, Bishop Robinson touched sensitive Protestant nerves. No doubt he spoke for many when, commenting on his reaction to discussions between secular humanists and Christians, he said, "I catch myself realizing that most of my sympathies are on the humanist's side. This is not in the least because my faith or commitment is in doubt, but because I share instinctively with him his inability to accept the scheme of thought and mould of religion within which alone that Faith is being offered to him. I feel he is *right* to rebel against it, and I am increasingly uncomfortable that 'orthodoxy' should be identified with it." [3] (A considerable number of Catholics, let me mention here, could say something similar.)

Of course many Protestants rejected out of hand what Bishop Robinson said. But it seems hard to deny that since

[2] New York: Sheed & Ward, 1961.
[3] *Honest to God*, p. 8.

World War II Protestantism has undergone a profound shaking of the foundations. The loss of cultural dominance is a sign of this change. In America, the Protestant ethos, bequeathed to the nation by the early Protestant settlers and the Founding Fathers, has been challenged and perhaps now overcome by the rise in Catholic, Jewish, and secularist minorities. The rejection by the Supreme Court of required prayers and Bible reading in the public schools can plausibly be seen, for instance, not as a death blow to religion in America but rather as a death blow to any identification of Americanism and Protestantism. In England, the fortunes of the Established Church have suffered enormous blows. That church has almost lost the working class, suffering grievously because of its identification with the aristocratic and monied classes. For the English intelligentsia, the established church is a dying symbol of a discredited set of superstitions. Even within the church, as Canon A. R. Vidler pointed out in his introduction to *Objections to Christian Belief*, there are those who "maybe for years, have been living with one foot in Christian belief and the other resolutely planted in the radical unbelief of the contemporary world, so that they are, as it were, torn between the two." [4]

In Germany, where the Evangelical Church had held sway since the days of the Reformation, Protestantism began to decline in the late nineteenth century, a decline which accelerated just before World War II. First it lost the intellectuals: to Communism, to Socialism, to secular humanism. Then, with the war, it managed (along with the Catholic Church) to compromise itself by failing to speak with force against Nazism; thus it almost lost beyond recall whatever vestige of spiritual power it may once have had to serve

[4] Philadelphia: J. B. Lippincott, 1963, p. 8.

as a conscience of society. Further north, the established
churches in the Scandinavian nations suffered a comparable
loss of power even where they retained the official support of
the state. In those nations, the churches became little more
than relics of another era.

Yet there was life. Many perceptive Protestants could
see well enough what was happening to the churches and to
Christian belief. One theologian after another called Protestants to account. They thrust their theological spears into
what they saw to be the pretensions of a comfortable, but
dying, Protestant life. Though from different perspectives,
and often in opposition to each other, they forced the
churches to take a hard look at themselves and the individual
Protestant to probe hard at the nature of his commitment.
The result was unsettling. Forced to confront their faith
afresh, many Protestants have come to believe that much
which they once accepted was little more than a culture religion. They found that traditional theism did not speak to
them, and they turned to Karl Barth or Paul Tillich. They
found that their former cultural dominance was little more
than a way of slowly killing the church, and thus a Reinhold
Niebuhr and a Dietrich Bonhoeffer suggested alternative roles
for the church. Some found that the Bible, far from making
life more intelligible, seemed to speak in the accents of ages
long past and from a metaphysical and scientific perspective
which seemed incredibly naïve. Rudolf Bultmann spoke to
their problem. But while these men gave Protestants new insights, they often shattered their private religious worlds as
well. So, in a sense, did the World Council of Churches when
it gradually came to cast aside any suggestion that a variety of
churches, often at creedal war with each other, was necessarily a sign of Christian vitality. The World Council's efforts

to bring the churches together forced them to look more closely at what they individually affirmed, making many realize that some of the most cherished confessional affirmations may represent only a narrow, complacent provincialism. The Second Vatican Council brought many Protestants up against the fact that the Catholic Church they had inveighed against for centuries was not necessarily the Catholic Church of the present day. One more prop of Protestant self-identification was weakened.

Bishop Robinson's book caught the quest for a new identity at a critical moment. It said in direct language that the Christian must now be honest with himself. He must admit that the old beliefs and traditions no longer have their old power. So it was that Bishop Robinson could state that his purpose was "to plead for the recognition that those who believe their share in the total apologetic task of the Church to be a radical questioning of the established 'religious frame' should be accepted no less as genuine and, in the long run equally necessary, defenders of the Faith." Yet he felt compelled to add: "But I am not sanguine. I am inclined to think that the gulf must grow wider before it is bridged and that there will be an increasing alienation, both within the ranks of the Church and outside it, between those whose basic recipe is the mixture as before (however revitalized) and those who feel compelled above all to be honest *wherever* it may lead them." [5]

The Relevance of Honesty in the Church

It may at once be asked: What is the pertinence of the Protestant search for honesty in a discussion of honesty in the

[5] *Honest to God*, p. 9.

Catholic Church? In answer, it is possible to say that despite the great gulf which still separates Protestantism and Catholicism, both have developed along remarkably parallel lines since the Reformation, and both have exerted some subtle influences on the other. Each went through a long period of framing much of its theology in reaction to the other. Each saw an outburst of mysticism in the late sixteenth and the seventeenth centuries. Each felt the impact of the Higher Criticism in the nineteenth century. Each had its bout with Modernism and theological liberalism in the late nineteenth and early twentieth centuries. Each saw, though in different ways, a reaction against liberalism. Each felt, in recent decades, a simultaneous impulse toward Christian unity. Most significantly, each experienced the same impact of modern European history, and has been alarmed by it: the rise of science and technology, democracy and socialism, the emergence of agnostic humanism, the development of the totalitarian state, the competition of ideologies, the revolution of depth psychology, the coming of positivism, existentialism, and linguistic analysis.

These parallels and this sharing of Western development mean that Protestantism and Catholicism rarely have wholly different problems (though they may often appear different). It would be astounding if Catholics did not now feel many of the same powerful impulses to greater honesty which are today moving through Protestantism. If not in America, at least in Europe the Catholic Church has had to confront the loss of cultural hegemony in some lands (such as France), and the rise of hostile ideologies in others (Communism in Italy and in Eastern Europe).

Even in America, where the Church has come into its own, it can no longer count on a pervasive Christian ethos to undergird its values. In the pluralistic setting which provides the context of most of Western Catholicism today, the Catholic is exposed to a variety of countervalues. The individual Catholic, no longer set in a Catholic milieu, must in an important sense take his faith with utmost seriousness if he is to be a member of the Church at all. Exposed from every side to philosophies and ways of life which challenge his, he can no longer survive by a mere conformity to communal values. Nor can he survive by a mere unthinking conformity to Church law. Now he must think and now he must make radical decisions. Now he must know what is at stake in his commitment to the Church. Now he must know how to distinguish what is essential in his belief from what is only a product of time and dispensable custom. Now he must have the courage to face his own worries, the honesty to admit them, and the zeal to resolve them. If he does not have these virtues, society will squeeze his religion out of him bit by bit. This it can do not only by blatantly suppressing him but also by leading him to think that his religion is part and parcel of his patriotism, but has no significance as a radically different way of life. This society can also do by subtly urging him to make religion a separate province of life, whose relevance to social, political, and economic questions is peripheral at most.

More deeply still, it is all but impossible to live with unresolved religious problems in a pluralistic society. A person who is not able to admit his difficulties to himself is bound to suffer from a spiritual and moral paralysis. Should he attempt to rest his personal integrity on a blind faith he will have to do so at a great psychological and intellectual cost. There are serious challenges to belief in the contemporary world; they can be ignored only at the price of dishonesty. Science, psychology, and sociology have shown that much once explained from a purely theological point of view can now be explained with equal plausibility from a naturalistic or deterministic perspective. To wish these new perspectives out of existence, or to leave them for the Church to sort out, is to risk personal disaster.

Life in a pluralistic society provides, then, one goad to honesty. Still another has been forced upon the Church by the great upheaval of the Second Vatican Council. When first announced by Pope John XXIII in 1959, the Council was seen as an opportunity for the Church to renew itself. If one of its ultimate aims was to create a more favorable climate for ecumenical dialogue, Pope John wisely recognized that this could be achieved only by an intense effort at renewal within the Church. The course of the Council itself actually encompasses two stories. The most obvious one has to do with the particular issues debated, the decrees legislated, and the shifting tides of opinion among the Council Fathers. Far less obvious, however, has been the revolution wrought by the Council on the Catholic consciousness. But it is a revolution of immense importance, the consequences of which may affect the Church in the future considerably more than any specific decrees issued by the Council.

A Promise of Freedom

Some might care to describe this revolution as the emergence of a search for freedom in the Church. Yet to say this is not to say enough because it was common in the past history of the Church for the Catholic to feel that he already possessed freedom. He understood the binding authority of the Church not as the bondage of slavery but, rather, as the freedom which springs from a total commitment to the authoritative voice of Christian truth. Thus it was taken for granted that the Church should suppress dissident opinion, that it should deal firmly with its undocile sons, that it should seek to nip any novel opinions in the bud. The Council brought this whole frame of thinking into question. It did this not so much because of any direct assaults on the authority of the magisterium of the Church—for there were no such radical assaults—but because of a wisespread recognition that rigid adherence to the old understanding of Catholic freedom is inadequate. It has proved to be inadequate because it stifled the possibility of free speech in the Church. Too many theologians, whose views were censored, maligned, or condemned prior to the Council, were proved right by the trend of conciliar thinking. The early troubles of an Yves Congar, an Henri de Lubac, a Karl Rahner could only appear, in retrospect, as symptoms of a dangerous sickness. How can such dangers be avoided in the future? No one yet has a clear answer to this question, but the fruits of experience now appear: the expression of a free conscience, however shocking to the status quo, must find an atmosphere of acceptance in the Church. Bluntly, this means that courage—on the part of the articulate individual and on the part of the listening Church—must replace mechanical docility. The principal fact of the revolution of freedom in the Church is that precisely this is beginning to happen.

This less obvious revolution also carries with it a growing awareness that if the individual is to have greater freedom of speech within the Church, he must also have a greater sense of personal freedom in thinking about the Church. The former freedom will have little meaning without the latter. Should anyone be prone to assert here that the freedom to think freely has never been in doubt, he would be under-estimating the kind of impact an excessively authoritarian conception of the Church can have on a man's conscience. An educational system which stresses humility and submissive-ness, which leads the individual always to assume he must be in the wrong if he questions authority, and which impresses upon him day in and day out the superiority of its wisdom to his, can have no other effect than to emasculate personal re-sponsibility. It cannot fail to make it difficult, if not impossi-ble, for a person to confront his own convictions honestly. In the end, he will not know what he thinks. He will only know what he ought to think—and that is not the same thing at all.

The Council has done much to call such an education into question. By its very emphasis upon "renewal" in the Church, a stress which often shaded off to the stronger word "reform," it conceded that the Church, in its human manifes-tations, is not perfect. It confessed, in effect, that it had made mistakes in the past. It all but conceded that mistakes are being made at present. Thus the myth of certainty was dealt a blow from which it could not recover. In a sense, the reactionary worries have turned out to be correct. Once one raises the possibility that all is not right in the Church, the way is open to throw almost everything into question. What the reactionary could not see was that that risk must be run.

The consequences of this development are now seen on all sides. Problems calmly accepted in the opening months of the Council have taken on a new urgency. Viewpoints which had only a subterranean existence a few years ago are now on public display. This was probably inevitable, for once Catho-lics got a taste of freedom, after perhaps a lifetime of con-cealed worries and speculations, it was only a matter of time before its full possibilities would be explored. The rapidity with which Catholic thought is now changing on the birth-control problem is the best indication of this. For years, many laymen and theologians stifled their misgivings about the co-gency of the Church's position on family limitation. The Church had spoken, and that was that. But with the freer atmosphere brought on by the Council, these misgivings came into the open, and with them a greater freedom on the part of theologians to re-examine what had previously been taken as irreformable doctrine. The same has happened to the questions of clerical celibacy, the prior censorship of books, the freedom of priests, and the right of dissent within the Church. Few of these discussions were envisaged by the Council Fathers in the early days, but they cropped up any-way and cannot now be stopped. The Council Fathers not only raised questions of their own. Both directly and indi-rectly they caused almost everyone else to raise questions. As time has passed, newer and more unexpected issues have appeared at an accelerating pace. They arise, for some, simply from new hopes and the possibility of new directions. For others, they arise because illusions have been shattered. For most, it is probably the combination of the two forces. Either way there is no turning back.

Something more needs to be said. Though it would be difficult to gauge their number, there are many Catholics today who find themselves painfully distressed with much they see in the Church, and with much they take the Church to stand for. They find themselves living in an age which challenges, with vigor and not always without integrity, much of the system of Catholic thought. They can observe well enough that it is a system which was framed in another day and that the self-evidence it once seemed to carry so unmistakably is apparent no longer. Yet it is not so much that they have come to reject the system: they find that they cannot respond to it with fervor, that it illuminates less and less of their life. It speaks to them in accents they cannot comprehend and presents them with "truths" which they find irrelevant to their own needs and those of their times.

Still, though they may see the irrelevance of much they were once taught, they can also see the myriad new directions in the Church. Though they can resent their earlier lack of freedom, they can also see the present increase of freedom. Though they can see that many of the old theological arguments are defective, if not sophistical, they can also see that many bishops and theologians (who once promoted these arguments) have now themselves come to reject them. Hope is sustained, and with just enough basis in concrete developments to make it meaningful.

Fear and Trembling

At the same time, despite much heady talk about the compatibility of Catholicism and freedom, of Christian truth and scientific truth, of the Church and the modern world, many Catholics can also see that these relationships have yet to be worked out in any detail. The optimistic syntheses still remain generalizations, often enough full of insoluble dilemmas at the level of daily life. How can such Catholics fail to be bundles of conflicting impulses and emotions: elated by the Council; dejected by the vestiges of the past; enthused by the new freedom; rebuffed by the presence of old suppressions? They await the final fruits of the Church's effort at renewal with fear and trembling: much depends on it.

Let me go even further. It is well worth considering the possibility that many who profess to be secure in their faith and only concerned that the Church be effective "in the world" are in fact in the throes of a basic crisis of faith. When they say they want the Church to be more relevant to the "needs of the contemporary world," they may really be saying they want it to be more relevant to them. When they say that the modern world no longer finds the Church's message meaningful, they may actually be saying that it has become meaningless to them. When they say that modern man finds it almost impossible to accept traditional Christian claims, they may really be saying that they themselves find such acceptance hard. It is as if many Catholics, fearful of admitting that their faith is at stake, disguise (even from themselves) the real problem by talking of the Church in the world. A personal crisis is projected to the less unsettling level of the Church's apostolic mission.

It would be a mistake to suggest that it is possible to sort out and neatly categorize the various responses the present generation is making to the world and the Church. Any such categorization would be an abstraction only, insensitive to the combinations and permutations which exist in the minds and emotions of today's Catholics. Let it suffice to say that the new spirit engendered by the Council and by the various currents (surface and subterranean) which now run through the Church are forcing the Catholic to confront his own belief as never before. Existence in a pluralistic society both reinforces and stimulates this confrontation. Personal integrity is at stake. If the Catholic does not know where his personal center lies, he knows he must find it. It cannot be located for him by others.

If nothing else, the fresh recognition that faith is an

encounter with Christ, not the mechanical assent to a set of abstract truths, forces the Christian today to take a new look at himself. He may easily convince himself that he believes the truths presented to him by the Church are worthy of acceptance. He may easily convince himself that the Church teaches in Christ's name and that the presence of the Holy Spirit will keep it from misleading him. He may be persuaded that the historical evidence supports the claims Christ made; that it supports the claims the Church makes; that it supports the efficacy of Christianity throughout time. But these things in themselves do not constitute an encounter, a living meeting, with Christ. They merely provide helpful conditions for such a meeting; one can recognize their existence without knowing the reality to which they point.

The recognition of this difference, between what one ought to believe and what one does in fact believe, is the very heart of the problem of honesty. Considerable courage is needed even to admit to oneself that there is a difference. Still more is needed to face up to its consequences. The Catholic today is being driven to this task, and a painful one it is. When he is not even certain what he ought to believe—for that is a distinct possibility during a period of transition in the Church—and not certain what he does believe, the magnitude of his personal struggle for integrity can be almost overwhelming. Hold on to Christ! Hold on to the Church! That is good advice, but who is Christ for me? What is the Church for me? These are the root questions of our day.

A Passion for Wholeness

It has been asked why, all of a sudden, so many Catholics have begun to stress honesty, authenticity, and integrity. The spirit of the times supplies one reason: it is a characteristic quest of contemporary man. More concretely, however, the contemporary Catholic is coming, finally, to take a careful look at the Church. He knows now what goes on behind the scenes, but unlike his predecessors, who may have known this also, he refuses to cover it up. He will not be a part of contrived advertising campaigns. He will not hush up scandals to preserve the good name of the Church. He will not accept at face value bland assurances that all is well. He will justify the Church before the world only to the extent it can be justified, not hesitating to destroy a favorable impression of the Church should he know it to be false. He will feel a positive obsession to expose myths about the Church, to point his finger at hypocrisy, to deflate overinflated reputations, to say the emperor is naked.

At the moment this obsession is, for a great many, an all-consuming one. But its source is rarely maliciousness, nor is it a love of scandal and gossip. It is a passion for wholeness, a drive to get to the heart of oneself as a Catholic. Pretense in the Church makes those who take part in it divided men. The true self is obscured, perhaps ignored, for the sake of the Church's reputation. The self, which should be rooted in authentic commitment and a firm grasp of Christian reality—Christ—is instead reduced to the playing of deadly games. It is forced by custom and convention to act out parts which have been superimposed upon it. The supreme virtue is taken to be the effacement of self, the denying of one's own insights, one's own response to the Holy Spirit, one's own creation of a meaningful Christian life. This is an intolerable demand, not because egoistical self-direction is a good to be sought, but because such a conception of self-effacement stands in the way of discovery of the source of selfhood. It is the inchoate recognition of this, I believe, which explains much of the restlessness among Catholics today. Despite all the talk of renewal, despite the many concrete changes taking place, the Catholic may be more confused today than ever. He is often at war with himself, at war with those in authority, at war with other Catholics. He may no longer know who he is: the landmarks of his earlier Catholic self-identity are disappearing from sight.

The words of a French Dominican are perceptively to the point:

In the midst of the anguish which is so common in our time, or in the face of the deep attraction of tangible, immediate fulfillment, the believer today suffers more than ever the temptation of disbelief. It is present as a promise of liberty. It is present as a call to unity, a call to whatever separates from life. It is present sometimes in the form of despair but more often in the form of exaltation. This strange attraction to disbelief proceeds not from what is most base but what is most elevated in man. Now all the more or less empty traditions, all the narrowness, all the useless moralisms, all of the theological and apologetical refusals to grapple with reality, all of the infantile fears of those in authority, from which a religious society rids itself only with great difficulty, render disbelief even more attractive.[6]

[6] Christian Duquoc, O.P., "The Mission of the Laity," *Perspectives*, IX (July–Aug., 1964), 116.

CHAPTER TWO

Public Dishonesty

Tʜɪs chapter and the following one will not be pleasant
reading. Their aim will be to set forth, as graphically as possible, some types and sources of Catholic dishonesty: in the
public life of the Church, first of all, and then in the private
life of the individual believer. In many ways, such a distinction is artificial. The public life of the Church is normally an
important index to the inner life of those who compose its
corporate body. Private dishonesty contributes to public dishonesty. By the same token, public dishonesty stimulates private dishonesty. It is useful, nonetheless, to approach the two
sources separately.

A protest is at once likely here. How can one pretend to
talk about Catholic dishonesty without first defining the
word "honest"? That is, at first glance, a point well taken.
The only trouble is that if one looks, say, to a standard dictionary for guidance there is little insight to be gained.
"Honest": "1. honorable in principles, intentions, and actions; upright; . . . 2. showing uprightness and fairness;
. . . 3. open; sincere; . . . 4. genuine or unadulterated;
. . . 5. chaste or virtuous. . . ." For synonyms, the following words are offered: "fair, just, incorruptible, trusty,
trustworthy, truthful, . . . straightforward, frank, candid.

. . ." The difficulties here are obvious: a person may be perfectly "upright" without being "candid"; or he may be "incorruptible" without being "open"; or "honorable in principles, intentions, and actions" yet not "frank."

But then one should not, after all, expect a dictionary to offer much guidance in a matter of this kind. Another acceptable method, usually more helpful, is for a writer to specify what he means by a word; that way, at least, some of the confusion and vagaries of unwanted connotations may be avoided. That will be the method followed here, except that I will reveal my definition by pointing to some examples of dishonesty. It is comparatively easier to observe those ways of language, disposition, and conduct which somehow produce a false ring than it is to discern those which are genuine. The belief that one has the ability to do this, of course, presupposes that one possesses at least a rough, working notion of honesty. Rather than attempt at this point a rounded definition of Catholic honesty, I would prefer to let my notion emerge gradually from the kinds of examples of dishonesty I note. Something more should be said here. The mere cataloguing of instances of dishonesty would still not take us very far. More importantly, it will be necessary to look at some of the motives and sources of dishonesty. That may help, I hope, to bring out the dynamism of dishonesty and thus prepare the way for a more positive look at honesty itself.

Forms of Public Dishonesty

Let us look first at the matter of public dishonesty. By such dishonesty I mean those acts of pretense, dissimulation, and direct distortions of the truth whose end is to serve the

Church. The important thing about such acts is that the individual who commits them does not do so for his own advantage. He commits them solely because he believes they will,
in some sense, contribute to the good of the Church. There
are many occasions on which deception may appear called
for. The most obvious is when the Church is under attack
and there is some element of truth in the accusation. There
may then be an overwhelming temptation to deny flatly the
charge in question, out of a belief that even to concede a
grain of truth would be to weaken the Church. So it was that
for centuries the Inquisition was passionately defended for
the care and precision of its juridical procedures and for the
purity of its purposes. Occasions of attack are not, however,
the only stimuli of public dishonesty. One may also be
tempted when it appears that some "higher" interest of the
Church would be furthered; or when a doctrinal or canonical
position would be enhanced in the eyes of the public; or when
a reputation might be embellished; or when some tactical end
could be served.

Now while it might appear that those who hold office in
the Church would be the most prone to such temptations,
this is by no means exclusively the case. Those who do have
authority—popes, bishops, pastors, lay leaders (in some cases)
—will generally be more concerned with the public appearance and the "interests" of the Church than those who do
not. Yet because of the nature of the loyalty of the Catholic
to his Church the temptation to public dishonesty is one
which can afflict any person. The most anonymous layman
can, when *his* Church is attacked by the most anonymous
critic, feel compelled to rush to the colors. To defend the
reputation of his mother or his wife, a man may feel that any
evasion of the truth is justified. So also, on occasion, he may

seek to protect the Church by some judicious bits of deceit. I should at once point out here that dishonesty of this kind need not be wholly conscious. It is a common enough human failing that when a man's religion or family are involved, the perception of the borderline between truth and falsehood becomes difficult to discern. Some qualities of character which we would consider admirable in the abstract may, in the particular, provide the main obstacles to perfect honesty. Where total dedication and loyalty to others are involved, it can be exceedingly difficult to admit even to oneself that a lie is a lie.

Whether the deceit is conscious or unconscious, however, there can be little doubt that much dissimulation is carried out in the name of the Church. Outright, conscious, blatant lies are, I trust, relatively rare and need not detain us. Only the most insensitive Catholic could manage them with a clear conscience. It is the more subtle forms of evasion and subterfuge which are of practical importance, those which are easier either to justify to oneself or to avoid noticing in oneself altogether. Without suggesting that any one form is more common than another, some of the more prominent are worth recording:

1. *Selective presentation of facts.* Since the Church is large, peopled with many diverse personalities, old in its history and complex in its life and structure, it is not at all difficult to choose judiciously those "facts" which most tend to support a given case or aim. This has been done time and again in presenting interpretations of the Church's history and of particular actions of the Church and its members. If one's purpose is to show that the Church has been a defender of the downtrodden, innumerable instances could be cited in support of the thesis. Should the matter under dispute be

religious liberty, case after case of Catholic toleration of non-Catholics could be drawn upon for verification of the Church's virtue. Was the Church in the forefront of the struggle for racial equality? Indeed, yes—for did not Bishop X invite Negroes into his schools in 1878? Did not Bishop Y condemn racists in 1937? Did not hierarchy Z issue a strong statement? By the method, then, of citing numerous positive instances to bear out a thesis, it can be made to seem impregnable.

2. *Glossing over weaknesses.* To be fully effective, the selective presentation of facts will normally have to be accompanied by a systematic minimizing of negative instances. This can be done directly by ignoring such instances altogether. But since that can be dangerous, the tactic is all the more effective if the counterinstances are acknowledged but the impression given that they are, at most, only exceptions proving the rule. The negative facts are made to seem inconsequential, of so little weight in the face of the positive ones that only those of ill-will would care to make much of them. Did not the Church persecute Galileo? To be sure, certain churchmen acted in a fearful, high-handed way, but the Pope made no solemn pronouncement on the case, and anyway when one considers the epoch-making work of the medieval universities, the innumerable great Catholic scientists, surely no one could claim that the Church has been anything but a great defender of science, and so forth. Or the matter may be one of freedom of conscience. Is it not true that Protestants in Spain and parts of Latin American have been denied the free exercise of their religion? Well, the answer often goes, "in a sense" this may seem true. But as a matter of fact it is not the freedom of their conscience which has been hindered but rather their doubtful right to engage in offensive proselytizing in traditionally Catholic areas.

Moreover, these are rather special cases, much more a matter of unusual historical circumstances and special cultural factors than of any theological significance. When placed over against what St. Thomas said about freedom of conscience (ignoring his views on the burning of heretics), against what the Church Fathers, the councils, and the popes have ever affirmed about the rights of conscience, and against the acceptance of constitutional democracy by Catholics in the overwhelming majority of countries—well then *surely* no man of equitable judgment would make much of what happened last week in Madrid or last month in some provincial court in Italy, etc.

3. *Prudential reasons.* Let us imagine a situation in which, even after the negative facts have been minimized or carefully set in isolation, they still remain embarrassing. Should we not assume then that perhaps those responsible had good reasons for their conduct, reasons not apparent to the outside observer? Is it not sometimes true that those in authority know things which others do not, and which they are not free to reveal? If Bishop A censures Priest Z, on grounds that seem wholly inadequate or unjust, must we not then give the bishop the benefit of the doubt, presuming that he must see facets of the matter which escape our eye? Or if hierarchy B refuses to take an open, unmistakable stand against some clear moral evil, should we not then trust to the wisdom of their decision, guessing that they must be subject to pressures which moral zealots cannot comprehend?

The persuasiveness of this line of defense rests on the fact that it *is* often difficult to know all the relevant considerations in particular cases. There will almost always be facts to which the outsider cannot have easy access. Nor will the outsider, precisely because he is an outsider, be able to see a

situation from the same perspective as those who have to
make the decisions. Taken together, such legitimate considerations provide a ready-made line of defense, one which
can be exploited almost indefinitely. It is a defense, moreover, which has the advantage of appearing to be based on
charity and which is compatible with the kind of respect for
authority expected of the Catholic. Its supreme tactical value
is that it usually places the critic in a bad light. If he persists
in his questioning, if he is unwilling to accept proffered ex-
planations, then he is open to the charge that he lacks charity,
that he assumes the worst about authority and that he egois-
tically believes he has some special moral wisdom. The burden of proof is thus always placed on the shoulders of the
dissenter.

4. *Good intentions.* There are times when an escape to
the hidden prudential reasons of those making decisions will
not work. Occasionally the facts, all of them, will become
public knowledge. When this happens, it is still possible to
obscure the issues by insisting on the good will of those responsible. Thus, the argument may run, even if they did—
perhaps—make a mistake, they were at any rate serving the
Church according to their best lights. Was Father L harshly
silenced by Cardinal P? Yes, but Cardinal P undoubtedly
was trying to preserve good order; there was nothing vindic-
tive or tyrannical about the suppression; it was for the sake of
the Church. By such tactics the impression is conveyed that
when errors are committed, the only thing that really counts
is the good intention of those committing them, and that if
excesses are perpetrated in a spirit of holy zeal, they should
be forgiven and forgotten. Again, this is a tactic which puts
the critic on the defensive, making him feel that any dwelling
on the substance of the matter rather than on the subjective

intention of those he criticizes is an offense against charity.

5. *The service of a higher truth.* When all else fails, a promising approach still remains—to set everything in a "broader context" or to see things in the light of a "higher truth." Scholar H, let us say, has been silenced by his superiors, though it is well known that his scholarship has won widespread support among those competent to judge its worth. One rationale may be that his views have disturbed the faith of many and that authority must take such considerations into account. Or it may be pointed out that his views have caused unpleasant dissension. He was silenced, then, not because what he said was necessarily false, but because it was the duty of higher authority to protect the equanimity of the faithful and to preserve unity in the Church. These concerns must take precedence. The merit of this argument is that those who protest the suppression are placed in the role of fanatics: they would imperil simple believers or Church unity just to see a point of scholarship accepted at once. In an analogous fashion it is sometimes argued that in those Catholic areas where effective religious freedom does not exist, it is the obligation of authority to weigh the impact on the masses of a sudden freedom for Protestants. Since that impact might well be devastating, and not correctly understood, religious freedom should be curtailed until the people are prepared for it.

Reverence and Image-Making

There are many other forms of subtle deceit. Evasiveness is a common one. When a direct question is asked, a vague, inconclusive answer is given. Or an answer may be given which attempts to play upon sentiment, deflecting the inquirer's attention. This is especially helpful when the actions of some revered figure are brought into question. It can then be argued that any missteps upon his part would be highly unlikely and that it is almost a calumny to entertain doubts. In itself, the great reverence which the Catholic feels toward the hierarchy affords that body a protection from pointed queries about its specific lines of action.

Deception, in brief, comes in many forms. Some are efficient by themselves. Others combine many tactics, each carefully deployed to create the desired effect. The net result is that of a hard truth concealed, of a favorable impression conveyed, of error transmuted into wisdom, of narrow-mindedness transformed into holy prudence. On the whole, the clergy manage deception more efficiently than the laity, who have less occasion to practice it. But the laity often equal them in determination when opportunity presents itself.

There is one category of dissimulators who deserve special mention, for in them the art of public dishonesty in the Church reaches its highest pitch. Like most other important institutions in the world, the Church has many members whose primary concern is the public image of the Church. They may be called the "image managers." They are those men and women, of high rank and low, whose work it is to present to the public (whether Catholic or non-Catholic) the best face of the Church. Sometimes this work is done much in the manner of, say, a governmental press secretary or a public relations officer. They do not conceive their task as that of providing a critical analysis of the actions of their superiors; instead, they simply convey, by word or tone or a combination of both, the impression which their superior wishes to see publicized. The telltale sign of their vocation is that they will never admit their private attitudes; and if they are skilled at their work, it will be impossible even to guess what they may secretly think. Sometimes this type of work is carried out by chancery office figures, by diocesan newspaper editors, and by specially delegated individuals. The important point is that they are consummately loyal, discreet to perfection, and totally unwilling ever to suggest that all may not be right with the Church. By a felicitous management of words and nuance, they know how to cover up conflicts, to hide flaws, to polish masks to a high glow. They are especially talented in the use of ecclesiastical rhetoric.

However common such figures may be in the Church there is one thing to be said for them. They only do formally what almost every Catholic has done informally at one time or another. Could any of us claim that we have never done a little image-managing on behalf of the Church? Could any of us claim that we have never tried to put the Church in a better light than the truth warranted?

Motives for Public Dishonesty

If it is granted that the forms of dishonesty just outlined do exist in the Church, it is necessary next to locate the motives which lie behind them. Since the very nature of the Church demands that it give full witness to the truth, why should a Catholic ever feel impelled to resort to falsehood to further its good name or to defend it against its critics? Why should there ever be a reluctance to tell the whole truth, to avoid whatever is misleading?

I have already suggested one basic motive: that which springs from a very human, and normally laudable, tendency to protect what we love. The mother of a hardened criminal who still insists "he's a good boy" is almost a stock figure. But

she is just as real a person as the Catholic who finds himself
constitutionally unable to admit in public that the Church is
anything less than perfect. Such a person always has a ready
explanation for any apparent deficiency. More often than
not, he is easily able to convince himself of the validity of this
explanation. What counts for him is the ultimate truth and
meaning of the Church; anything which challenges the value
of his dedication must necessarily be repulsed. The good
name of the loved one is his constant concern.

This motive, which springs from an emotional rather
than a rational loyalty, would not be so powerful if it did not
feed on other motives which operate in the Church. One of
these is a false piety. Since it is an article of faith that the
Church is holy—because its source was holy and it remains
under the protection of the Holy Spirit—it is easy for the
Catholic to conclude that he has an obligation to minimize, if
not deny, anything which might suggest the contrary. To be
sure, few in the Church would suggest that one has such a
duty. But, by the same token, very few authorities have ever
urged Catholics to take special care to be scrupulously candid
about the realities of the Church. The overwhelming emphasis in Catholic teaching, whether of a popular or an advanced
variety, is on the goodness of the Church. This is a pillar of
the faith, one of such persuasiveness that a Catholic will almost naturally shy away from doing or saying anything
which might weaken its solidity. It is natural to conclude that
there may be moments when the Church is best served by a
deliberate refusal to concede any flaw. This is particularly
true when a Catholic has been raised to believe (as many
have been) that the world is ever ready to think the worst of
the Church, to misunderstand it, and to seize on the slightest
sign of weakness to press home its attack. It will be very hard

to convince the person who feels this way that he should be
frank with "outsiders." Nothing is harder than to tell the
truth when the truth may be used against one.

The kind of false piety which leads the Catholic to conceal the truth from outsiders has an analogue within the
Church. It is summed up in the concept "offensive to pious
ears." For example, theologians have often been refused per-
mission to publish even theologically orthodox conclusions,
or to popularize them, because of the possibility that they
would unsettle the piety of the simple faithful. Moreover, the
concept has even broader applications. It can provide a convenient pretext to withhold information from the faithful. It
can offer a handy excuse for an informed Catholic to keep his
less enlightened brethren in the dark about some aspect of
Catholic life. For those privy to state secrets, it can furnish a
ready-made excuse to conceal errors, injustices, stupidity, self-
seeking, and venality. The assumption is that the simple believer will be better off if his illusions remain intact. It is thus
for his own good that—by the unilateral decision of those who
know—he is denied some point of truth.

Why this way of thinking has rarely been challenged is
difficult to understand. To the extent that truth is withheld
for the sake of the sensibilities of simple believers, their belief
is (to that degree) misguided. It is a way of saying that it is
better to have an idealized conception of the Church, or some
doctrine of the Church, than a true conception. It is also a
way of saying that faith is something which should be preserved from the rough edges of reality; and this amounts to
saying that faith should have no contact with the world as it
is, with men as they are. For the theologian who is forced to
take sensibilities into account, there is a strong inducement
to modify his insights, to put them into a language which

conceals the thrust of an argument, to veil the truth behind a
screen of words which denatures their impact and power of
clarification. But whether it is the case of a bishop discreetly
hiding the full truth, or a theologian evading the risk of
speaking in an open way, or simply one layman failing to
dispel the illusions of another, the result is the same: the
power of myth is enhanced, that of truth lessened.

Another common motive for public dishonesty lies in a
desire to protect the dignity of an office by covering up the
faults of those who hold the office. Though the practice is
perhaps less rampant today than in the past, it is still custom-
ary to create an aura of sentimental piety around a person in
high office, suggesting ever so delicately that the man in the
office is specially worthy of it. This is normally the task of
those around him. By their exaggerated deference, their dot-
ing on his words, their efforts to protect him from whatever
may be awkward or less than dignified, they can effectively
present him to the public, reasonably certain that his private
foibles will not be visible. By their attitudes and actions they
can also set a standard of respectful deference, setting the
tone of his encounters with the public, making it exceedingly
difficult for the lowly to establish any kind of relationship
with authority other than that desired by his retinue. The
latter can be counted upon to make extraordinary efforts to
protect the reputation of authority, by elaborate defenses of
his conduct, by constant and effulgent praise of his virtues, by
careful efforts to see that nothing happens which might reveal authority in a light different from the one desired.
Again, however, all this can be done by any Catholic if the
occasion presents itself. An official retinue is aided in its work
by anyone who feels that piety and respect demand that the

person and his authority always be made to seem like the perfect marriage of man and office.

Closely related to this impulse is the great respect which Catholics normally have for the past. The Church does have a glorious past, perhaps the greatest in the Western world. It can count heroic martyrs, holy popes, bishops, priests, nuns, brothers, and laymen. It can boast of valiant struggles against hostile powers. None of this can be denied. Nor can it be denied that the constant faith of the Church is an equally important source of Catholic doctrine. Because these things are true, it becomes possible to romanticize history, either by endowing every decision of the past with a special wisdom or by acting as if it was nothing but one triumph after another. The motive is to instill in the faithful a sense of the Church's continuing glory, to reinforce assent to doctrines and practices whose origins are remote, to place the contemporary actions of authority in a context which immediately identifies them with the victories and wisdom of past ages. A richly furbished heritage is evoked as an indirect means of defending the present. The one thing incompatible with such an evocation is an admission that the past also had its disasters, shortcomings, and misdirections. For the moment it is admitted that the Church has been known on occasion to fail in its high task, it then becomes possible to wonder if the Church is failing now. By forestalling this kind of speculation, an awesome respect for the present can easily be maintained.

Another motive for dishonesty is the pervasive belief that it is always healthier for a Catholic to develop the habit of thinking only positive thoughts about the Church. Dwelling on the weaknesses of the Church and its members is often held to be destructive of piety or wholehearted commitment. Insofar as the emphasis falls on the word "dwelling" this is probably a valid psychological observation. Nonetheless, the Catholic has as great a duty to admit in public the faults of the Church as he does to help others approach it in a spirit of positive affection. It is a matter of balance, of candidly confessing faults while also calling attention to genuine virtues. In this manner a rational respect is encouraged, one which accords with reality. The Church, least of all, should tolerate the kind of process which, under the heading "the power of positive thinking," would condition men to train their minds and wills systematically to suppress whatever is unfavorable to the Church.

A final motive for dishonesty (though many others of less importance could be mentioned) concerns the Church's status in society. Both the Catholic and the Protestant churches are blessed and trapped in the free world by their high social and political status. They are blessed in that they do not have to cope with outright persecution. They are blessed in the homage paid them by politicians, in the tax benefits they receive, in the deference given to their priests and ministers. This is, unfortunately, also a snare. The price which the Catholic Church has had to pay for its physical, social, and economic security is high. On innumerable occasions it has muted its prophetic role, paying heed instead to local sentiment and mores, the sensitivities of financial supporters, and the good will of secular officialdom. It has sought the favor of the press, the acceptance of non-Catholics, the benevolence of the well-heeled business community. At times, it has used its secular influence to coerce those who opposed it. Above all, it has kept its ears attuned to the winds of public opinion in society, retreating when expedient, pushing forward when the moment was propitious. By no means has it acted immorally; but it has done what is, for the Church, almost as bad: it has conformed itself to the expectations of the culture, steering clear of a witness which would disturb its community standing. By so doing, it has been led to dwell too much on its appearance, too much on its worldly status, too much on its good name; it has, inevitably, courted dishonesty.

Tools for Dishonesty

So far I have discussed a few forms of public dishonesty in the Church and have tried to suggest some of the more common motives behind them. It is now time to take a look at those Catholic habits, forms of life, and means of expression which make the perpetration of dishonesty possible. Even for the most determined, it will not ordinarily be possible to deceive others unless there lie close at hand tools with which to fashion the desired image. In a trivial sense, it is easy to be dishonest: one can simply say No when the truth requires Yes; or plead ignorance when knowledge is possessed; or change the subject when a direct reply is called for. Other than a quick mind, no special tools are necessary for such pedestrian deceits. The trouble, however, with using such primitive tools is that it becomes at once apparent to the user that he is engaging in deceit; moreover, it may be comparatively easy for the one deceived, on careful investigation, to expose the deception. Far safer and more promising are tools for deceit which are elaborate, those which enable one to hide the truth in a verbal jungle, mingling truth and falsehood in an impenetrable way. It is far easier to defend a

friend's angry temper by portraying him as an emotional, spir-
ited, volatile figure (implying lovable qualities) than by
flatly denying that he has an angry temper.

There exist in the Church many complex means of car-
rying off a deceitful witness. Most of these means are neutral
in themselves. It is a question not of what they are taken to
be in the abstract but of the kinds of uses to which they can
be put. In many cases they are essentially good things capable
of being put to bad use. I stress these points in advance because, in almost every case, it will be possible to object that I
seem to be willfully distorting something that is good or that
at least need not be understood in the way in which I will
present it. I grant this, though I hope it will seem an unnecessary objection by the time I am through.

We may begin, first, with the rhetoric employed by
many members of the Church, ranging from popes to pastors
to lay functionaries, both past and present. The most characteristic place in which this rhetoric is found is in authoritative documents of the magisterium—conciliar statements, papal pronouncements, episcopal utterances; but the same kind
of language is often used in sermons and on ceremonial occasions. The predominant note in this rhetoric is its elaborate
reliance on a conventional set of pious words and phrases. It
is a stylized language, sometimes solemn as in the case of
magisterial documents, sometimes richly metaphorical and
allusive when used for less important purposes. On occasion
it may bear the clear stamp of its author; but more commonly
only an acute reader could note stylistic quirks. It is in a
sense a timeless style, sometimes making it difficult to determine (leaving aside considerations of content) whether it
was written in the eighteenth or the twentieth century, by a
liberal or a conservative, by a person or a committee. It is,

moreover, a style which often leaves unclear whether words are being used to state facts, to exhort, to arouse emotions, or to prescribe acceptable attitudes of mind—or perhaps being used for all of these purposes at the same time.

But if the usage of words in such rhetoric is not always clear, its rhythm usually is. Short, direct sentences are rare. Instead, clause is joined to clause, each following the other in the methodical unfolding of a point. In one encyclical we find, almost without trying, a sentence like this: "When new and serious difficulties and questions were arising, at times from the widespread prejudice of *rationalism* and at times particularly from the discovery and investigation of the antiquities of the East, this same Predecessor of Ours, moved by the zeal of his Apostolic Office not only in order that such an excellent source of Catholic revelation . . ." and so on for nearly eighty words more. This brief fragment of a quotation serves also to illustrate two other typical characteristics: "rationalism," for example, is called a "prejudice," thus demeaning those who may in fact hold such a philosophy out of careful conviction. The "Predecessor" in question was moved by "zeal," thus typifying an invariable tendency (regardless of who the predecessor might have been) to extol the motives behind the works of the past and those responsible for them. More often than not, predecessors are men of "immortal memory" or "happy memory." If a pronouncement is directed at patriarchs, primates, archbishops, bishops, and local ordinaries, they are addressed as "venerable."

It is of course obvious that these phrases are simply a matter of long-cherished pious usages. They comprise a convention which normally pays homage to the past, thus setting any contemporary pronouncement in a context that joins it with whatever else may have been said on the same subject.

No less a part of the convention is the painting of earlier pronouncements in the most vivid hues, even when—and perhaps especially when—a departure is being made from those pronouncements. There can be no denying that conventions of this kind have their good uses. They help to show, by style alone, the unity of the Church through time. They help to encourage due respect for the achievements of ages long gone. They provide a common vehicle for the expression of concepts, reflections, and teachings, which can readily be grasped by divers men in divers situations (assuming they have been educated in the convention). They help to minimize the idiosyncratic and the eccentric, and to obviate the necessity of creating new forms of language with each passing generation. Churchmen, no less than lawyers or diplomats, find such conventions of pragmatic value.

The great weakness in relying upon them, however, is that they lend themselves, on the one hand, to abuse. They make it easier to conceal one's real purpose in speaking. They make it easier to avoid direct statements. They make it easier, for the purpose of evasion, to blanket what one is saying with a massive onslaught of words. They make it possible to say absolutely nothing while appearing to say something of significance. They make it possible to conceal a steel fist beneath a velvet glove. They enable one to play games with words and with meanings. Conventional rhetoric has been used for all of these purposes in the Church.

On the other hand, the conventional rhetoric of the Church has some more subtle liabilities. Since it is a language heavily weighted with varied and rich means of praising the Church, and no less varied and rich means of condemning forces or ideas out of favor with the Church, it is ill-adapted to the expression of humility and repentance. The gingerly way in which the word "reform" was treated in the early months of the Second Vatican Council is a case in point. Here was a word, standing for a cluster of concepts, which simply had no place in the conventional rhetoric of recent centuries. Those who dared to use it ran the risk of appearing to be under the sway of Protestantism. The word "renewal" appeared far safer, free of any radical connotations. Yet it also had the drawback that it did not express forcefully the urgency of the work before the Church; it suggested that only a bit of sprucing-up was necessary. In contrast, the idea of "reform" places the matter in a clearer light. As Hans Küng has pointed out, the word *reformare* had a perfectly legitimate meaning: "to give another form," "to restore an earlier, better form," "to form something anew that has been deformed," "to shape something according to its own essential being." [1] Even so, it has remained a word which Catholics approach at arm's length. At most, "reform *in* the Church" is an acceptable expression, while "reform *of* the Church" is not, thus neglecting the possibility that a full implementation of the former might in practice amount to the latter.

My point is that if the Catholic is to have full freedom to acknowledge the sins of those in the Church, to criticize its shortcomings, and to press for a reanimation of moribund institutions, he needs a language in which to do it. This he does not possess in the conventional rhetoric; it was not developed with that possibility in mind. He is forced to grope for words, to have recourse to the vernacular or to obscure phrases drawn from ancient eras of Church history. The result is that he is almost foredoomed to be misunderstood. He will look like one—to use a word from the conventional vocabulary—given to "novelties." Concretely, common Catho-

---

[1] *The Council, Reform and Reunion* (New York: Sheed & Ward, 1961), p. 9.

lic parlance does not have the linguistic tools to criticize a pope; to take charitable exception to episcopal pronouncements; to state directly that the Church has made a mistake or failed in some essential duty. One can say no more than language allows one to say: there are many things that the shortcomings of Catholic language render inexpressible. It is this fact, I would speculate, which helps explain the sense of frustration felt by many who see glaring weaknesses in the contemporary Church. They see things which they cannot express in traditional terms, and therefore find themselves in a psychological state similar to that of a child in a preverbal stage of development—forced to rage within and mutter inarticulately in the face of parental shortcomings.

A second potential tool for dishonesty is the common practice of describing the Church solely in terms of its celestial garb. It is never easy for the Catholic to confess that his Church bears the wounds of the humanity of its members, but it is all the more difficult for him to do so because he is given few theological means to understand the interaction of divinity and humanity in the Church. Day in and day out he will hear of the glories of the Church. He will be given a thorough education in the claims of the Church, in the marks of the Church, in the infinite superiority of the Church to all other churches and institutions. The Church he will hear of will be, in the main, a Church of theological abstractions. He will rarely hear of the Church imbedded in time and history, subject to all the influences of relative cultural values, passing fashions, political forces, intellectual biases and the frailties of man. As Bishop Stephen Laszlo of Eisenstadt, Austria, observed in a speech to the assembled fathers at the Second Vatican Council, "The Church cannot be understood except as the eschatological people of God, on pilgrimage through time, proclaiming the death and resurrection of the Lord until He comes. . . . But this eschatological pilgrimage is often understood too abstractly. . . . Men of this world often point out that the concrete Church is very different from the Church described by theologians and preachers. Theology seems to describe the Church as *saints*, but life itself seems to show us a Church of *sinners*." [2]

Since this important problem will be discussed at some length in Chapter 5, it will suffice for the moment to mention one possibility of dishonesty to which theological abstractions on the Church can lend themselves. That is the possibility they afford to blur the difference between principle and practice in the Church. Should it be said, for instance, that "the Church opposes racial discrimination," what does this mean? Does it mean only that the theologians and magisterium of the Church have taught that racial discrimination is sinful, an affront to God who is the God of all men? Or does it mean that the Church, understood as the whole community of the faithful, shows in its actual behavior a consistent opposition to discrimination? Clearly an affirmative answer to the first question will not entail an affirmative answer to the second. But what counts here: what the Church teaches or what the Church does? An abstract answer would base itself on the doctrine of the Church; a concrete answer would look to the interaction of doctrine and behavior. When the Church presents itself triumphantly, however, little is heard of the actual inclinations which conduct reveals. Even less is heard when the Church feels called upon to defend itself from criticism for specific practices.

[2] "Sin in the Holy Church of God," in *Council Speeches of Vatican II*, eds. Hans Küng, Yves Congar, O.P., and Daniel J. O'Hanlon, S.J. (New York: Paulist Press, 1964), pp. 44–45.

If it is said, for example, that such and such a Catholic hospital practices (or once practiced) segregation, it can be replied that one should not be misled by appearances since it is well known that the Bishop of the local diocese has firmly stated that segregation is wrong and that the Church has always opposed racial injustice. What actually happens in the Church is, in short, made to seem beside the point, as if the only thing that matters is what the Church teaches. Since it is perfectly possible to find almost every human evil solemnly condemned in some important magisterial pronouncement, a ready-made protestation of *ultimate* virtue is almost always easy to document. Another way of putting this is to say that the traditional ways in which the Church is described make it relatively easy to confuse the "ought" and the "is." Catholics *ought* to be true Christians; that is essential to their faith. But to say this is not by any means to assert that every Catholic *is,* in his daily life, a true Christian. Yet since the Church is so often discussed in ideal terms only, it is easy to infer that ideal and reality are one in the Catholic's thinking about the Church. Or again, since the Church by its own conventional self-description *ought* to be perfect, it is easy to reply to the skeptic that the Church *is* perfect—if only the skeptic would cast off his blinders and see it properly.

A Non-Confessing Church

A third potential tool for dishonesty is, in many ways, the most important, for it provides a handle for the two already mentioned. I am thinking here of that informal but nonetheless real tradition that the Church does not publicly confess its failures and mistakes. On occasion, to be sure, a pope has admitted that the Church has done things worthy of blame. But this is quite rare, and even when such admissions are made they are usually vague and general. This is not to deny that many individual bishops and theologians have confessed sins on the part of the Church. Yet that is very different from solemn confessions on the part of the magisterium. There is no tradition in the Church which provides for, much less encourages, such confessions; the actual tradition (in an empirical rather than theological sense) militates against them. It is this fact which ultimately explains why there is so little conventional rhetoric capable of adequately expressing an awareness of guilt discerned by the Church; and also why almost all of those descriptions of the Church which are common coin heavily stress an idealized holiness of the Church.

In the best of all possible worlds, the lack of such a tradition would be of little consequence. But in our world it provides a very dangerous potential source of dishonesty. I want to call special attention here to the inducement it provides to rationalize the conduct and policies of the Church. If it is taken for granted (in fact if not in theory) that the solemn teaching authority of the Church should not openly repudiate its mistakes, then the scholar and theologian in the service of the Church is inevitably under pressure to devise rationalizations for the Church's conduct. He will make certain that it is never caught in so tight a corner that the only honorable way out would be for it to beat its breast in repentance. He will find ways for the Church to save face.

Many possible strategies can be brought to bear here. One of the most common may be called the "historical-context" strategy. Pope Pius IX's *Syllabus of Errors,* for instance, is a highly embarrassing document for anyone who would argue that the Church should be counted among the

defenders of religious liberty. Similarly, Leo XIII's en-
cyclicals provide rather awkward obstacles to the claim that
the Church has ever defended democratic liberties and a free
press. However, for the ingenious exegete of papal documents
there is no problem: once these documents are seen in the
context of nineteenth-century anticlericalism, secular rationalism, and agnostic individualism, it becomes obvious (does
it not?) that much of what they contain has no relevance to
the contemporary situation. There is thus no need for the
Church to repudiate some of the more offensive points enun-
ciated by Pius IX and Leo XIII. These points had pertinence
only when they were uttered. The infinite possibilities inherent in this kind of approach are being amply exploited today.

Another strategy is afforded by the "development of doctrine." The history of theological thought on the moral licit-
ness of sexual intercourse apart from procreative purposes,
for example, is highly erratic. Up until at least the seventeenth century there was a strong body of theological opinion, dating back to St. Augustine, which held that a nonpro-
creative use of sexual relations between man and wife was at
least a venial sin. More broadly, it was assumed for centuries that sexual intercourse was almost by its nature something especially tainted with original sin. But does the existence of such a strong theological tradition cause any embar-
rassment to the contemporary theologian intent on showing
the inherent goodness of sexual relations? Not at all, for it is
well known that "new insights" are constantly being discovered which throw old teachings into "a new perspective."
These insights provide a "deepening" of Christian thought.
Put this way there is no need to publicly declare that a wrong-
headed strain of theological thought once distorted the thinking of countless generations and that the Church did nothing

to uproot such thinking. All that is necessary is to show that the theologians have changed their opinions and that, once again, the freshness of the Church's theological vitality has been demonstrated.

It may at once be objected here that this is an unduly jaundiced way of looking at two perfectly valid principles of Catholic scholarship. Papal and episcopal pronouncements *are* written in historical contexts. It is perfectly fitting and proper that Catholic doctrine should undergo development; after all, the Holy Spirit is ever active in the Church. I readily grant these points. My intention is only to show how principles perfectly legitimate in themselves can be misused for the purpose of making it unnecessary for the Church ever to have to admit that it made mistakes. To show the power of a historical context is to offer an explanation of a text; this is valid enough. But when, as so often happens, an explanation is allowed to function subtly as an excuse, then dishonesty can creep in. Again, it is one thing to assert that Catholic doctrine develops but quite another to present this development as simply a matter of constant enrichment. For it often turns out that the enrichment in question involves the positive rejection of something accepted in the past. It is good that this should be possible but it is dishonest to act as if the past is not being rejected; to act, that is, as if doctrine always develops in a smooth, well-oiled fashion, moving from good insights to better ones. As often as not, good insights have replaced bad ones; and sometimes bad ones have replaced good ones. The Church is now not only understanding the Reformation better, but is also coming to see that it often positively misunderstood it. The same can be said of sexuality, of the nature of the state, of private property, and of the role of the layman. Even so, it is still unheard of for the magisterium to give chapter and verse when alluding to its past misdirections (such allusions are, of course, rare enough anyway).

Church Authority and Human Power

The final potential tool for dishonesty to which I would call attention concerns the role of authority in the Church. Theologically understood, those who hold authority do so for the sake of service to God and to the Church. Authority derives its role, its mandate, and its efficacy from God; hence it is wholly dependent upon God and subordinate to His supreme authority as Lord of Church and world. The obedience that ecclesiastical authority commands is a religious obedience, not an ordinary human obedience. Moreover, those who give assent to this authority, the people of God who make up the Church, must do so freely. The relationship which holds between those who command and those who are commanded is a moral relationship, not one based on political, social, or physical coercion. Authority is accepted, ideally, because of a recognition that it derives from God and that it is ordered to service.

Unfortunately, these truths are sometimes lost sight of. Authority is then glorified as if it had a human meaning independent of its spiritual meaning; or as if positions of authority are held by virtue of some personal charism stemming from worldly talents and strengths. This kind of glorification is obviously wrong and deserves no special attention here. What is more pertinent is that, for many centuries, the Church has been prone to present authority in such a way that it partakes of the general awe and respect accorded men in high places. While the theme of service may be amply stressed, the actual image of authority which makes its appearance on the public scene is of a worldly power. It is a power that *appears* to have no hesitation about resorting to those time-honored devices by which powerful men create an aura of importance about their person: a cultivation of titles and formal modes of address; an unwillingness to appear in public unless the setting of their appearance is carefully arranged to preserve and enhance their dignity; a reluctance to be caught unprepared; a hesitation to place themselves in situations where their authority may be subjected to slights or challenge. The motive in each instance is to do nothing which might destroy the atmosphere of authority, and everything which might enhance it. Small wonder, when such motives are operating, that the vital idea of authority as a service is lost sight of. It is not always easy to discern a servant in a man who is garbed in princely robes, who is surrounded by a retinue of functionaries, who is called "his excellency," "his holiness," "his eminence," who commands police escorts, who frequently has the same privileges in society as presidents and kings. It is possible, but difficult.

These modes of deportment, address, and courtly trappings are not necessarily incompatible with humility. Ample experience has taught the Church that. Nor are they incompatible with honesty. Yet they are a potential source of dishonesty. Above all, they tend to obscure the humanity of authority, subtly conveying the impression that Church authorities have a human wisdom which others do not possess. In this way the ground is prepared for habitually giving authority the benefit of doubt, and not just of an ordinary kind, but of a kind which presumes that authority must always be wiser than others. To the extent that this actually happens, a false impression will be given, one which effectively projects a misleading image of the person of authority: an image not of service but of an omnipotent prince who cannot be easily approached, who cannot be a man among men, who cannot profit from the wisdom of those he rules.

Let me propose a rule of thumb. Whenever authority *appears* to be something other than it is, the way is opened for dishonesty. In many instances, authority has no control over its appearance, which may be the result (and usually is) of customs long antedating those persons who hold office at present. But insofar as authority cultivates these customs, using them to create conditioned psychological responses in others, great harm can be done. Usually, it is not difficult to manipulate ordinary men. But precisely because it is not, those in a position to do so have a special responsibility to avoid anything which would actually bring manipulation into play. Men are easily awed by a show of pomp and power. They will give unthinking, un-Catholic obedience to those who know how to play upon that awe, responding not out of filial respect in a spirit of moral freedom but because the trappings of power evoke an automatic conformity. In the end, then, a false response is given to a false appearance. Authority is false to its own nature just as the respect given that authority is of the wrong kind and for wrong motives.

CHAPTER THREE

Private Dishonesty

ACCORDING to a common stereotype, the Catholic as a believer is a whole man. Unlike the Protestant, supposedly, he does not pick and choose those Christian truths which he will accept. Unlike the agnostic, purportedly, he does not fashion a philosophy of life out of eclectic material drawn from this quarter or that. By his adherence to the authority of the Church, it is said, the Catholic is one for whom doubts do not exist, difficulties and contrarieties do not arise, and painful probings and uncertainties have no place. It is for this reason that Catholicism is sometimes likened to a totalitarian system, a system which rests on the shoulders of true believers whose devotion to their theological truth banishes the ordinary complexities of life.

Such a conception of the Catholic is a false myth. Yet despite what some observers may think, it is a myth which could not exist were there not many elements of Church life which seem to deny that it is possible for a Catholic to be troubled. One source of this myth lies in the way his belief is often presented: the Catholic is supposed to be distinguishable from other men by his absolute certainty, his unwavering devotion, his secure conviction that his search for truth has come to an end. The individual Catholic often enough does his part to sustain this preconception. To the outsider he will present a solid presence, one which carefully conceals any problems he may be having. Even to other Catholics, he may not fully reveal himself; his inner restlessness will be masked consistently and effectively.

In hard fact, however, the Catholic may be as much subject to uncertainties as the next man. This is particularly true today. For the past decade the Church has been in the midst of a tremendous upheaval. Many practices once thought permanent have been called into question by the Second Vatican Council. Many teachings, once thought unquestionable, have been subject to intense analysis and criticism. Many hesitations, once carefully hidden, have now come into the open. While much of this rumbling is the natural fruit of a desire for renewal in the Church, it has also unmistakably revealed the existence of a subterranean life in the Church which is far more complex than the bland surface that appears in theology manuals. The real drama of the contemporary Church, it could well be said, is not a new confrontation with the "world," but rather a gradual awareness that this subterranean life must be faced.

It is a life with many hidden streams, some more obvious than others. Among the more easily discernible are those currents of contemporary theology which are responsible for calling into question an excessively legalistic conception of the Church. For some years prior to the Council a number of theologians were quietly attempting to find new ways of getting at the reality of the Church. Most commonly, they turned to the Bible: at once they found that the biblical imagery of the Church was both richer and more meaningful than the juridical concepts favored by an older generation of ecclesiologists. Gradually their work has found its way into the public life of the Church, though the process of evolution has been slow and is still incomplete. The same could be said of moral theology. Here it was a question of bringing the Church to see that Christian ethics is something more than a deductive system of moral prescriptions indistinguishable from theorems of a moral geometry. It is, instead, a whole way of life, open to possibility, demanding personal freedom, encouraging responsible decision. The insights making possible this shift were drawn, again, from the Bible along with the discoveries springing from phenomenology, existentialism, and personalism.

Far less apparent, however, is that current which carries with it problems concerning the freedom of the Catholic to explore his own conscience and consciousness. Once even the slightest possibility was raised that past conceptions of the Church could be misleading or downright inaccurate, then the way was opened for the Catholic to begin asking himself some hard questions. Among them are: When I say *credo ecclesiam,* to what am I committing myself? Do I, in fact, believe everything the Church supposedly requires me to believe? How free am I to raise questions, to pose difficulties, to suspend belief about this or that point of Catholic doctrine? These have become pressing questions in the contemporary Church. Although unavoidable, they are not questions with which a Catholic can feel at ease. Much of the training and conditioning which a Catholic receives is of a kind to induce him to be wary of exploring his own beliefs—which may not coincide with those demanded of him by the Church— directly and courageously.

Public dishonesty in the Church is designed to conceal the truth from others. Private dishonesty is designed to conceal the truth from oneself. It is this latter dishonesty which I now want to explore. For if it is in fact true that the Catholic today must be willing to examine his faith afresh, both to preserve its integrity and to give it a new vitality, then it is first necessary to look at those obstacles existing within the Church which make it difficult for him to do so. Why is it so painful for him to inquire into the solidity of his faith? to ask himself whether he believes what the Church says he must believe? to admit to himself that a certain doctrine does not convince him? Why, in brief, is he subject to the temptation of private dishonesty, a dishonesty which is willing to settle for the appearance of Christian selfhood and not its reality?

The Dangers of Authority

Whatever else may be said of the Church, it is impossible to deny that Catholicism is an authoritarian religion. Understood theologically, this fact poses no special problem. The Church rests its claim to teach and to guide on the mandate given it by Christ. That right, which resides most fully in the hands of the popes and bishops, has as its task the preservation of the deposit of faith, the instruction of the faithful, and the formulation of those laws and practices deemed necessary to strengthen the Catholic and the structure of the Church. By definition, the Catholic is one who accepts this authority, freely submitting himself to its dominion. In return for this submission he has the assurance that he is following the will of God and will not be led astray in his understanding of God and the Church. It is the duty of those who hold office to exercise it not for the sake of their personal glorification but in the service of God and truth.

Thus understood, the authority of the Church cannot be seen as in any sense a form of tyranny. On the contrary, it is meant to be a source of freedom and self-liberation. It provides freedom by showing man a way out of the closed circle of finite existence, by releasing him from the captivity of the false and the illusory, by putting him in contact with the perfect ground of all freedom, God. It is meant to liberate him from the transitory by showing him the way to the eternal; to liberate his mind and emotions from a solipsistic bondage to self by joining him with the ground of full selfhood; to liberate his thinking from the tutelage of a world where truth is too often trod underfoot. Through the Church, God effects the salvation of the world. Through the Church, man finds his way to God. The Church speaks, instructs, and commands because that is the order Christ willed.

In some circumstances, however, the authority of the Church can pose a serious threat to individual integrity. This can happen in a number of ways. The primary threat lies in the way the Catholic is ordinarily introduced to the authority of the Church. Almost the first thing he learns as a child is that the Church possesses a complicated and demanding set of laws and prescriptions. He learns that he must attend Mass every Sunday and on designated holy days, that he must receive the sacrament of the Eucharist at least once a year, that he must not eat meat on Friday, and so forth. The purpose of these laws is to assist the Catholic to open himself to the grace of God. In themselves, they are capable of strengthening the Christian in his commitment to God. But the magisterium does not simply establish laws. It attaches to their violation various penalties, the severity of which depends upon the will of the Church. Hence at the very outset of his life an element of fear is introduced into the conscience of the Catholic, a fear which is often evoked by priests, nuns, and parents when they face a recalcitrant child. Authority does not say only: It is good to attend Mass every Sunday. It also says: You risk eternal damnation if you willfully refuse to attend.

The process of coercion does not stop there. If a child is not awed by the penalties of disobedience to Church law, then it is usually possible for the parents to coerce him in more directly tangible ways: by physical punishment or by the less violent methods of pressure available to them. If he attends a Catholic school, his teachers can also penalize him in various ways for failure to observe the law. While the point of such coercion is to impress upon the child the seriousness of his obligations as a Catholic, it is very easy (and frequently the case) for him to believe that external conformity alone is all that is required of him. It does not matter whether he wants to go to Mass, whether Mass has any meaning for him. What does count is that he be physically present. The inevitable result of such coercion is that an artificial wedge is driven between the child and his conscience, between the child and his personal integrity, between the child's private inclinations and his public behavior. When coercion is present there can be no question of the personal freedom of the child. He has only as much freedom to make his own religious decisions as those who have authority over him choose to allow. By rewards and punishments he is conditioned to respond the way his ecclesiastical elders and superiors want him to respond. He is taught to consider himself guilty if he does not conform.

But obedience to Church law hardly exhausts the matter. In his religious education, the Catholic child is commonly expected to learn the fundamental teachings of the Church. Toward this end he is instructed in a body of material which he is expected to master. From the child's perspective, however, what may count in this instruction is not whether the truths to which he is exposed come to have a personal meaning for him (though the teacher may hope this will happen), but whether he learns what he is supposed to know. To achieve this goal, he is usually graded as in any other subject and for poor work he may be punished by means of the various restrictive measures available to teachers. Conformity is the price he has to pay for the acceptance and good will of his mentors.

As a rule, there is little room for dissent in Catholic education on the lower levels (and frequently not even on the higher levels). The child is expected to be as docile and submissive in religion class as in arithmetic class. To ensure this docility, his religious education is accompanied by a thoroughgoing indoctrination in the etiquette and demeanor required of the layman in the presence of nuns and priests. He is taught to pay elaborate homage to the dignity and lofty status of those in the religious life. He will learn that normally it is not proper for him to challenge them, especially on religious matters. He will learn that deference to their religious authority, and the purported wisdom which goes with that authority, must be the norm to be followed at all times. What training cannot accomplish in this direction, the garb of nuns and the collar of the priest often can. These are signs of authority, signs that those so adorned are figures deserving of special respect. Since it is relatively rare for nuns in particular to set foot in the homes of those they teach (because of the regulations of most of the religious orders), the sense of distance between student and teacher is enhanced.

Finally, most Catholic primary and secondary education is triumphal in tone. The child is taught the glories of the

Church, its spiritual conquests and advances throughout history, its unique place among the religions of the world, its special right to merit total dedication in the name of God, its massive spiritual power, and its impregnable standing even in the secular world. Although it is easy to find theologians and spiritual writers who will talk of a Church of sinners, this is a note rarely heard in the common run of Catholic education. Only in his later years, if at all, will the student hear of these things. The end of this triumphal emphasis is to impress upon the child the uniform greatness of the Church; implicitly, if not explicitly, it also teaches him that only the prideful Catholic could dare raise questions about this greatness. The Church is an institution to which the child must totally adapt himself—of this he is left in no doubt.

Let me now interject a warning. What has just been said about Catholic education and Catholic training is, taken alone, unfair and misleading. It makes no allowance for the fact that much of this shaping and training is conducted in an atmosphere of charity and genuine concern for the spiritual welfare of the child. Nor does it take account of the fact that the pointing out to the child of the glory of the Church *ought* to be part of any decent religious education. That is part of the faith of the Church and cannot be neglected, just as it would be improper to suggest to a child that a priest or nun should not be respected. The difficulty here is one of balance. For it is perfectly possible, and often happens, that principles valid in themselves are instilled in such a way that the result is a conditioned person, one whose response to Catholic truths has become a matter of reflex actions, of habits of mind and will whose dynamism is not a rational and spiritual commitment but an adherence to the norms of others. To the extent that Catholic training engenders such conformity, the child is protected from self-confrontation. His selfhood is defined by those who train him, and only that self is recognized which shows itself amenable to the educational process. As an inevitable by-product, automatic group loyalty, aggressive solidarity, and a harsh treatment of the maverick in the community can be expected.

There can be little doubt that the historical setting of the Church at any given moment of history will have much to do with the way it directs its means of education. Like much of Western society until recently, the Church followed the prevailing view that the child had no rights whatsoever. When excessive corporal punishment was thought healthy, Catholic teachers had no hesitation about applying it. When absolute silence and submissiveness were expected of the child, the Church expected the same. Yet the Church also had additional problems which led it to place a heavy emphasis on eliciting from children instant obedience and reinforcing group conformity. As the cultural influence of the Church waned during the past century, it sought to preserve the child from the values of a hostile society by training him much as one would train a soldier. It does not appear to have emphasized the necessity of choice and free will in religious commitment—for some may have taken such an emphasis as license to do what they saw fit—but of a self-emptying responsiveness to law and precept. It did not often emphasize the necessity of an intelligent faith—for some may have confused the demands of reason with the permissiveness of secular rationalism—but of a blind faith. In these emphases it showed the effect of fear: the child was looked upon as a potential victim of the non-Catholic world. The only hope of saving him, it was believed, lay in an education which would psychologically minimize the choices available to him. He would be molded so thoroughly in mind and will that he would see the world only from the perspective of the Church. That spirit still lingers in the Church, though there are innumerable signs that it is beginning to die.

Difficulties and Doubts

Although a possibility, one does not ordinarily expect the young child to have serious difficulties, much less real doubts about the teachings of the Church. If they arise at all, they will come later, probably during late adolescence. How is the Catholic trained to deal with them? The first thing to be said is that while it is now generally accepted among educators and psychologists of religion that religious uncertainties are a normal part of growing up, it is still exceedingly rare for this perception to find public acceptance. Catholic secondary and collegiate education is customarily conducted as if the student were a perfect believer, serene in his faith. The educator may know better, but this does not necessarily mean he will be willing to accept as a matter of course that many of the things he says about the Church will not be accorded an eager hearing. There are many responses to this resistance. The sensitive teacher can be expected to handle student perplexities with delicacy. Those who are not sensitive will use different tactics: they may bully the student, pointing out how ill-equipped he is to think he could have problems which the Church has not solved. Such a teacher will undermine or destroy a student's self-confidence, ever reminding him of the great distance between the wisdom of the Church and his own finite, immature mind. Still another tactic is to assure the student that all is well, that he should just put his problems out of his mind: better to think about other things. Or he may be assured that it is perfectly natural to have difficulties: the truths of the Church are deep and mysterious. The only proviso is that he must not let these difficulties become doubts; should that happen he will be in great danger. Whatever the stratagem, the student is rarely urged to get to the bottom of his problem.

The reason for this wariness about difficulties is not hard to locate. The Catholic is expected to possess his faith in certainty; his adherence to the Church cannot be a provisional matter. That is why, presumably, a genuine, full-blown *doubt* about some article of faith is accounted by the Church as a serious sin. But this teaching is a ready-made trap for self-deception. As long as the Catholic believes that to doubt is to sin, he may have little motivation to press even difficulties very far: it is morally dangerous for him to do so—or so he may easily believe. But what if he should, in any case, have a doubt? Many remedies have been proposed by spiritual writers, of which prayer is the most prominent. Yet hardly less important, traditionally, is the advice given by one moral theologian: "Turn the mind away from the subject altogether." [1] As a piece of practical advice for security of mind, this may be a wise suggestion. But as a prescription for self-knowledge and self-understanding it is a dismal failure, little less than a blueprint for self-deceit. For a time it may work, and may even appear to strengthen a flagging faith. But in the long run, the suppression of serious doubts will eat away at the doubter's integrity. Sooner or later, he will recognize that he has been playing an elaborate game with himself. Once again, a wedge will have been driven between the self of external conformity and the real self.

[1] Henry Davis, S.J., *Moral and Pastoral Theology* (4 vols.; New York: Sheed & Ward, 1935), I, p. 293.

A further complication must be observed here. Catholic theology recognizes a sharp distinction between articles of faith and the customs and laws of the Church. Careful Catholic training will make this distinction clear. In many cases, however, it is easily lost sight of. From the perspective of the student it may appear as serious to doubt the wisdom of a particular piece of Church legislation as it is to doubt the Incarnation. If the Catholic must believe in the Incarnation in order to be a Catholic, he may think that he should also believe that Church law is always wise and prudent. Otherwise, he runs the risk of appearing out of step with the mind of the Church. Rebellion against ecclesiastical law is often as little tolerated as rebellion against central Christian truths; or so, at any rate, it may seem to the student.

It is easy to understand how this can happen. An important aim of Catholic training is to give the individual a comprehensive picture of the Church: its source in Christ, its historical development, the relationship between revelation and human law, the interaction of fundamental principles and those practices and customs in the Church designed to support those principles, and so on. Hopefully, the individual will come to look upon the Church as a harmonious whole. This is as it should be, but one almost inevitable effect is that the Church, in both its spiritual and human manifestations, appears to be a tightly interlocked system. One cannot, with such a system, challenge any given part without seeming to challenge the whole structure. A bishop, let us say, acting out of his legitimate authority decides not to issue a public statement on some controverted question of social morality. In most cases, there would be no reason why an individual Catholic could not criticize the bishop's decision as long as he did not call into question the right of the bishop to make de-

cisions. Yet should he do so, he in turn may be attacked on
the following grounds: the bishop has the right to make prudential decisions; to call his prudential decisions into question is to undermine the spirit of respect which the faithful
should accord a bishop; any act which undermines this respect is a threat to legitimate authority: therefore the critic
should remain silent. One might call this the tyranny of the
camel's-nose argument: take one step in the direction of challenging authority, even a theoretically permissible one, and
the way is opened for many further, more dangerous steps.
The camel's-nose argument looms large in Catholic contro-
versies, just as it will in any community where the system of
values is characterized by a close interrelationship of all the
parts to the whole. Important distinctions, crucial discrimi-
nations, and the difference between what is orthodox and
what is heterodox is likely to become blurred. Everything
seems to be of a piece. Pull one thread loose and the entire
tightly wound knot may unravel. In the Church, that is what
many Catholics too often believe. However unrealistic such
a view may be, it is nonetheless pervasive, effectively operating to persuade Catholics to soft-pedal any reservations they
may have about particular points of doctrine or practice.

The Protocols of Evasion

So far I have stressed the way many Catholics are led to
look upon their religion. Important as this formation is, however, the same forces which constitute its inner drive can continue to operate in the adult life of the Catholic. Whatever
his age, there is still too little in the actual life of the Church
to encourage the individual to bring his problems about the
Church into the open. There is equally little to encourage

him to admit them to himself. Years of hearing incessantly that the wisdom and standing of the Church are superior to those of the individual effectively ensures that anyone who does discern a problem will be prone to question not the Church but himself. He will have learned that any criticism may be interpreted by authority as a manifestation of pride or arrogance. He may have been led to believe that real difficulties about the Church are all but impossible for the Catholic of good conscience and humble disposition. He can easily believe that, when he has problems, they are probably a symptom of misunderstanding, of a defect of Christian character, of psychological misdirection, or of the harmful effects of the secularistic atmosphere of society. Though he may know that it is perfectly possible for the Holy Spirit to enlighten the individual in the Church—indeed, to raise up prophets to call the Church to account in particular circumstances—he is rarely given reason to believe that the Holy Spirit could be working through him, here and now. On the contrary, he may have been formed to believe that his judgments about the Church, when they are of a critical nature, are, most likely, temptations. The presumption is nearly always in favor of the status quo, rarely of the questioning individual. Knowing this, only the unusually bold are likely to raise questions; the rest are scared off by the forces arrayed against them. And the most effective censor lies within the self. The Catholic superego, formed over the years, instantly warns against the dangers of following one's private insights. Better to trust the Church. Better to trust authority. Better to trust the consensus of the community. Be docile, be submissive, be self-effacing: that is the safe way. True selfhood is achieved by perfect conformity. To doubt one's own insights, however carefully examined, is no sin. To doubt those of the Church may be—and often is.

One of the most dangerous consequences of this imbalance between the individual and the Church, between conscience and the weight of authority, is the encouragement it offers to concealing one's real thoughts from those in authority. It is a common quip that once a priest is appointed bishop he will never again hear the truth. Doubtless this is an exaggeration, but it contains a large measure of truth. As long as it is considered a potential threat to the excercise of episcopal authority to question the judgment of a bishop even on an isolated matter, the prudent Catholic may judge it wiser to remain silent. After all, who is he to doubt the value of the acts and thinking of a successor to the Apostles? Who is he to pretend to the possession of a Christian charism equal to that of a bishop? To conform one's thinking to that of one's bishop is accounted a virtue; to depart from his thinking can be a vice. For the priest this is especially important. He has the specific duty of serving his bishop and, in addition, promises him obedience in his ordination ceremony. Nowhere does law or custom require that a priest speak his mind candidly to a bishop. Nowhere is he exhorted to offer his opinions and his advice to his bishop. The priest's duty is obedience and cheerful service.

While the layman does not make a specific promise of obedience to his bishop, there is practically nothing in canon law which would give him a juridical right to dissent from a bishop's judgment, nor any encouragement to address complaints to him. One theologian has put the matter succinctly:

The bishop is the ruler, the shepherd sent by Christ to his territory. The layman is responsible for his own personal life. He must rule his own life as directed by the bishop who stands for Christ. He must follow the bishop's teaching in the domain of the natural law, in the moral aspects of the social and political spheres, in the area of canon law, even in the application of these laws of Christ to his own personal decisions. This is a true act of maturity. It is to rule one's life according to the will of Christ.[2]

In just what sense "the layman is responsible for his own personal life" is, to say the least, not apparent. As for canon law, the rights of the layman are hardly extensive, with no mention being made of any circumstances under which he would have the right to dissent from a legitimate command, or of any under which he would have the duty charitably to admonish a bishop (or a pope) who failed to live up to the requirements of his office.[3] None of this precludes the possibility that a bishop may personally be tolerant of criticism and correction, and be willing to accept advice and frank statements of opinion from those in his charge. Very many are. But the layman and the priest can claim few juridical rights in these respects.

What is true of the relationship between a layman and his bishop has analogues on other levels. The individual bishop is in somewhat the same position in relationship to the pope as a priest is to a bishop. Protocol stands in the way of a bishop's giving unsolicited advice or offering unasked for criticisms to a pope. On a lower level, the relationship of the layman to the priest is usually marked, unless they are friends, by a special show of deference on the part of the former toward

[2] Donald Dietz, O.M.I., "The Bishop and the Layman," *American Ecclesiastical Review*, CXLVII (Aug., 1962), 114.

[3] Cf. John F. Reed, S.J., "The Laity in Church Law," *Theological Studies*, XXIV (Dec., 1963), 602–625, for a valuable survey of the canonical rights of the layman.

the latter. There are no common-law traditions, much less canonically based ones, that specify the ways in which a priest must be deferential to the opinions of the laity. The laity, on the other hand, are generally well aware of the respect they owe to the clergy. Informally, there is nothing to prevent the laity from criticizing the clergy or speaking their minds to individual priests. But there is nothing in Church law or etiquette which provides for a formal opportunity to do so. The weight of authority is almost entirely on the side of the clergy.

In each of these relationships within the hierarchical pyramid, then, the lower is always subject to the higher (granting, to be sure, different meanings of "subject to" in each relational situation). In practice, this means that the person lower on the scale is dependent upon the good will of those superior to him. When to this inevitable consequence of the juridical structure of the Church is added the aura of special worthiness and virtue with which Catholics endow those of superior status, then directness and honesty by subordinates have comparatively little to support them. Even when there is no question of special authority, a whole host of conventions tend to keep the Catholic from speaking what is in him. Michael Novak has written that:

There is a conspiracy of gentility, politeness and adulation, which inhibits honest sentiment and direct speech; and these conventions carry over from the speakers' platform and the Catholic press to private conversations. A layman finds only a few priests or religious to whom he would confide the same convictions, doubts, criticisms he confides quite readily to other laymen. This conspiracy against candor is apparent to the impulsive and the naturally frank within the Catholic environment; and those who live outside that environment sense the air of quaintness, constraint, and less-than-truth as, on occasion, they are called back into it.[4]

As true as this undoubtedly is so far as the layman is concerned, it would be surprising if the same thing could not be said of the relationship of priest to bishop, of bishop to pope.

Stratagems for Security

The direction of Catholic education, I have observed, is toward the instilling of a total vision of the Church, with part related to part and each to the whole. This direction in turn reflects a permanent tendency in Catholic thought: toward the creation of a systematic body of knowledge and speculation. The guiding principle behind this tendency is, in part, a natural drive of men to see reality as a whole and to make sense of its different elements. There is nothing peculiarly Catholic about this drive. What is perhaps unique to Catholic thought is an unusually heavy emphasis on the principle that one truth cannot conflict with another. While few Western thinkers are likely to deny what is in one sense a verbal truism, Catholics are apt to lay special stress on the point. For it is an essential conviction of Catholics that God is the author of truth, and that God does not contradict Himself. Of almost equal significance is the conviction that God so protects the Church that, in matters of faith and morals, it will be preserved from teaching erroneous doctrine. As abstract principles, no Catholic will find any special difficulty here.

The deployment and application of these principles are another matter. If they are abused or misused, they provide

[4] "Nuns in the World," *The Commonweal*, LXXIX (Nov. 29, 1963), 275.

ready-made rationalizations for the perplexed mind. Let us see how this is possible. Take, as a random example, the problem of free will and determinism. The Church teaches that man has a free will, that he can exercise rational choice. Much of contemporary psychology, however, on the basis of some persuasive evidence, is inclined to argue that man is determined by his biological nature, his cultural environment, and by material conditions over which he has little control. Theoretically, it is not difficult for the Catholic to resolve these conflicting claims. Since the Church teaches that man has a free will, and since the Church is preserved from substantive error, then it follows that man's will is free. Given this conclusion, it must necessarily be the case that those psychologists who argue for determinism are wrong. But what of their "persuasive" evidence? Clearly it cannot be as persuasive as they think: it must, of necessity, be evidence which is misunderstood, or which springs from a false system of evaluating evidence. Yet suppose the Catholic cannot find any flaw in the evidence, but only in the conclusion to which it points? This need pose no real problem either. Since we know with absolute certainty by virtue of the authority of the Church that man's will is free, it becomes obvious that the methods in question deal with only a part of the total human person. It is then possible to say that the results may indeed be "true" at their own level—that, say, of empirical phenomena—but that this level must be placed in a broader context, and in *that* context they will show themselves to constitute only a partial truth. In sum, there must be an explanation of any apparent conflict of truths; we know, at the very outset, that any conflicts must always be only "apparent."

Is this elaborate process of reasoning merely a rationalization? Does it not suggest that there is no evidence which could ever be brought forward that would decisively show the Church's teaching on free will to be wrong? The answer is, in principle, No for the first question and Yes for the second. No other answers are possible if the Catholic is to be consistent with his religious beliefs. But that does not mean there is not a latent danger here. If the Catholic is to be intellectually honest he must confront the evidence which is brought forward. He must be willing to suffer in the face of the evidence. He must be willing to admit that there does appear to be a conflict of truths. He will be dishonest only if he denies the evidence without looking at it or if he ignores it even though he knows of the challenge it poses.

The pitfall in the abstract principle that there can be no conflict of truths is, then, that it can serve as a tranquilizer. One need never worry. One need never thrash about seeking a way of reconciling different truths. In particular, it provides a way for the Catholic to trick himself. Does he perceive a conflict? But, he has been assured, in the long run there can be no real conflict. Does he fail to see how this conflict can be resolved? But that does not matter since someone in the Church will surely find an "answer" sooner or later.

The theologian can be as tempted by easy answers as the ordinary man. Many theologians consider it their duty to find a rational basis for the Church's teachings or, if that is not possible, to find an ample basis in Scripture and tradition. That is a worthy goal, but it is one which, if care is not exercised, can easily degenerate into something akin to the work of political hacks whose job it is to provide arguments in favor of the party line or of pre-established doctrines. The mark of such men is that they never publicly admit to the existence of decisive counterarguments. They are loyal civil servants whose self-identity is achieved by their efforts to make the Church's position appear unassailable. As fast as one line of defense proves inadequate they prepare another. A twofold deception may be the end result: the ordinary believer can evade his own problems by casting them on the shoulders of "experts" and "specialists," trusting that they will find a way out for the Church. In turn, the specialists, having defined their own task as the finding of plausible solutions to knotty puzzles, will avoid any solution which might confirm the worries of the untutored. It is an uncommon theologian who will bluntly tell a troubled Catholic that there may be a basis for his perplexities.

No doubt it is common for authoritarian institutions to have various techniques of maintaining loyalty, of reassuring the skeptical, of controlling incipient revolutions, and of sustaining respect for authority. It would not be difficult for a social scientist to discover the techniques employed in the Church toward these ends. Naturally, the fact that the Catholic believes most of these "techniques" have divine sanction casts them in a different light for him; they will not seem to be "techniques" at all. But unless the Catholic is capable of observing how even perfectly valid principles of Church doctrine, polity, and discipline can have their manipulative side, he will be a potential victim of self-deception. The greatest single objection in the contemporary world against absolutist systems of belief, whether of a political, ideological, or religious nature, is that they force the individual to lie to himself, to shape his life and thought not according to his free conscience but according to the demands of the system. Nothing has told more heavily against Communism than the twists and turns of the loyal party member trying to justify the latest shift in Communist tactics. Whatever the party decrees is, by definition, right. Unless the Catholic is careful, it is easy for him to fall into the same way of thinking. He will fail to see that he remains responsible for his beliefs, and that this will hold true even though he is committed by his faith to trusting the Church through foul weather and fair. As soon as the Catholic attempts to side-step the tension inherent here, especially by an abdication of personal responsibility for his belief, he will be at odds with himself, prone to rationalize, to evade, to mouth reassuring clichés, to comfort himself with meaningless slogans. He will never know who he is and what he believes.

The Self-Deception of Progressives

Nothing, I think, would be more naïve than to assume that self-deception is possible only for certain types of minds in the Church. In the Church of Vatican II, caught up in the throes of the quest for renewal and reform, it is especially easy for the progressives to believe that they have a monopoly on honesty. A *prima facie* case might be made for such a claim. Have not the progressives been zealous in confessing the past sins of the Church? Have they not been the ones to point out the discrepancy between theory and practice? Have they not called for greater openness in conceding difficulties and unresolved problems in the Church? Have they not been candid in their admission that the Church was unduly harsh to the Protestant reformers? Have they not been willing to risk the security of that old-time Catholic religion in order to make the Church more open to new insights and doctrinal developments?

All of these things are, at least in my opinion, true. At the same time, these very virtues can cover some elaborate forms of self-deception, all the more subtle because they can

have the appearance of great candor. The most obvious form
of potential self-deception is to take for granted that one's
progressive spirit represents an unadulterated impulse toward a greater service of the Church. But as a matter of fact it
is perfectly possible for such an impulse to mask some serious
and unadmitted misgivings about the nature of the Church
or particular points of doctrine. Thus it is conceivable that a
desire for a more permissive exercise of authority in the
Church, one less absolutistic in its hold upon the individual,
can actually hide a serious doubt about the validity of any
kind of binding ecclesiastical authority. Since the latter alternative, if openly admitted to oneself, would amount to a
major crisis of belief, it is safer for one's spiritual security to
find relatively indirect ways of expressing one's reservations. It is, then, very convenient to make a distinction between the legitimacy of authority in the abstract and the
exercise of authority in the concrete. Every concrete act of
authority could be rejected as tyrannical or paternalistic or
insensitive to human freedom while, at the same time, being
conjoined with a defense of authority on the level of abstract
principle. (One is reminded here of the segregationist who
protests that he fully accepts the equality of the races but
who, in fact, objects to any measures which might effect inte-
gration.)

To take another possibility, it is possible to imagine
that some who press for the principle of collegiality in the
episcopal body could actually be using this as a self-deceiving
device for covering their doubts about papal primacy and
infallibility. Or that those who are not convinced that there
is a hell would instead attempt to persuade themselves that
there is no necessity of believing that there is anyone in hell.
Or that those doubtful about the historicity of important

parts of the New Testament would resort to emphasizing the "symbolic" meaning of the doubtful passages. Or that those in the midst of a personal crisis about the Church's prohibition of mechanical means of contraception would find themselves concerned with the "population explosion."

The point in each case would be to avoid any basic conflict where a choice might have to be made between remaining in communion with the Church and cutting oneself off from it. The avoidance would not have to take the form of creating fictitious solutions or arbitrarily stressing irrelevant points but of so emphasizing one legitimate aspect of a doctrine that the offending substance of it is effectively neutralized. What Karl Rahner says of "latent heresy" in the Church can be applied, *mutatis mutandis,* to the way an individual can deal with his personal problems:

Hence this latent heresy has two principal methods: on the one hand it avoids coming into conflict with the magisterium by avoiding clear statements in books, official teaching etc., and taking refuge in the private and esoteric domain reserved for the initiated only; on the other hand, it keeps to the vague and approximate, the undefined attitude, and in writing concerns itself only with the doubtful, with 'attempts,' and with the exposition of unsolved problems (but in fact meaning more than this), passing over truths which contradict it in silence. To put it more briefly: Heresy in the Church today (if it exists) must and can take cover, and by being indifferent in theory and fact to the truths of the Faith which contradict it, can remain latent in the Church.[5]

Here it could be said that any evasive strategy which it is possible to use in the public life of the Church is also capable of being used in one's private thinking about the Church.

[5] *Nature and Grace* (New York: Sheed & Ward, 1964), p. 71.

Used in the former way, one is safeguarded against open conflicts with the magisterium; used in the latter way, one is
safeguarded against open conflicts within the self.

Another source of self-deception for the progressive can
stem from the resentment he may harbor toward those men,
institutions, and customs which stand in the way of a re-
formed Church. Until very recently, the general lot of the
Catholic liberal was a hard one in the Church. He lived under a constant cloud, ever subject to disciplinary action, os-
tracism, censure, and suspicion. As a student he may have had
to contend with reactionary theologians whose attitudes and
rebuffs kept him constantly on the defensive. As a seminar-
ian, he may have engaged in constant struggles with his pro-
fessors, spiritual advisers, and seminary rector, the fate of his
vocation hanging in the balance. Expected to conform to the
local school of opinion, he may have been forced to hide his
own insights, to speak with great circumspection, and to compromise his own ideals (often drawn from wholly Catholic
sources). As a theologian, he may have been disciplined or
silenced. As a writer or an editor or a lay leader, the Catholic
liberal may have had to be wary, living in constant fear of
suppression. Although life has become easier for the Catholic
liberal since the advent of the era of the Second Vatican
Council, the necessity for a healthy sense of caution remains
in force.

An atmosphere of this kind inevitably breeds resentment. It becomes relatively easy to believe that one's own
cause and one's own values have a special merit: as if the
more opposition one encounters, the greater validity one's
stand must necessarily have. An ideal breeding ground for
self-deception is thus prepared. One form of self-deception is
to assume that one's cause could not possibly represent a

mere party spirit, an ideological counterthrust to forces whose main crime is that they have been sources of personal opposition. Another would be to assume that one's theological progressivism represented nothing but the pure promptings of the Holy Spirit, free of any self-seeking desire to see the forces of reaction obliterated. Indeed, one might be tempted to convince oneself that there was no question of "progressivism" at all but rather of a *true* conservatism, one intent on reinstating Christian values which have been destroyed by those who (falsely) think themselves "conservative." Resentment, then, can be a powerful psychological force, ever capable of leading one into a justification of self which exceeds the bounds of either truth or perfect honesty. That this resentment may be based on specific abuses does not change the matter. Too many men in the history of the world have deceived themselves and those around them while in pursuit of a redress of real injuries.

It is not impossible to observe within Catholic liberalism a phenomenon similar to that which affects others who have turned against an earlier total commitment. Each is prone to see only the worst in the system rejected. Horror stories, stories of persecution, injustice, stupidity, and pettiness abound in their private conversations and public utterances. They have a compulsion to expose the deceptions of the rejected system. Where they once saw dedication, they now see hypocrisy and venality, pride and arrogance. What they could once interpret in an edifying way, they can now view only in terms of baser motivations. They are given to seeing their earlier loyalty to the power structure as a case of an innocent person duped, a simple man full of ideals taken advantage of. They find it hard, and sometimes impossible, to recall the good qualities of those who once commanded their trust. To be sure, the Catholic liberal will continue to recognize that even the conservative thinkers he has come to reject still remain part of the Church, and are thus his brothers in Christ. The demands of Christian charity will set a further boundary to his bitterness. Even so, the fruits of dissillusionment often betray themselves. The liberal can be a person as smug and self-righteous in his new loyalties as he once was in his old.

The Self-Deception of Conservatives

For his part, the conservative may be subject to equally strong drives toward self-deception. Because he is likely to conceive himself as a protector of the ancient faith against the inroads of time and secularism, he will be given to imputing less than worthy motives to those who question whether every element of Catholic life is equally timeless. He takes his stand on the unchanging nature of the Church, holding that this is one of the great glories of the Church, a sign of its divine origin. But for him, the way to protect this truth (a truth which the Catholic liberal will share) is to remain indiscriminately faithful to whatever has been blessed by the past. A phrase such as "making the Church relevant to modern life" will be suspect for him. By its possession of truth, the Church is already relevant! To adapt the customs and laws of the Church to the mentality of contemporary man is to fall prey to the seductions of modernity. To concern oneself excessively with the Church's impact on the modern mind is to see the world through distorted lenses: it is the world which should be worried, not the Church. He may believe that the Catholic liberal must be a victim of his times, deluded by false prophets, captivated by dangerous modes of secular thought, weak and insecure in his confidence in the power of the Church.

The conservative is peculiarly apt to lay heavy stress on abstractions. It is not the Church as it exists empirically which captures his attention, but the Church of eternal verities. What the Church does is not as important as what the Church *is*. Indeed, what the Church does, at least in the matter of its failings, is something more or less accidental. When the Church fails, this failure has nothing to do with the essential nature of the Church. Neglecting to note that the Church is not just an idea, the conservative will attribute its shortcomings to weak Catholics—the Church never fails, though Catholics sometimes can; thus the Church is sharply distinguished from the community of believers. So it is also that false ideas are seen as the great enemies of the Church. Men would not fail if their minds were not captivated by the allure of base theories, strange ideologies, and godless thought. The way to protect the Catholic is to keep him from alien thinking. Not virtue but orthodoxy is the first requirement of the Catholic; not charity but truth; not reason but submission; not understanding but acceptance.

As a corollary to the latent heresy of the progressive, Karl Rahner speaks also of the latent heresy of those who proclaim their perfect orthodoxy:

But there is yet another form of . . . hidden heresy, and, paradoxically, it can affect those who are proudest of their long-standing and unimpeachable orthodoxy; heresy in the form of indifference. . . . [A] freezing of the form in which the truth of the Gospel is expressed is in fact a dangerous symptom of indifference, whether conscious or not, to the truth, the symptom of a lack of power to assimilate it existentially and express it in new terms. Who could doubt that this form of heresy also exists in our time—heresy in which dead orthodoxy is only the expression and the result of a secret indifference to the truth, in which a thing is left unchanged because men are so indifferent that they do not want to have to go to the trouble of getting rid of it or questioning it? [6]

One might add here that this "indifference" could also be a manifestation of a secret fear that the truths of the Church could not survive any attempts at a fresher expression or a new formulation; that they are too fragile and uncertain to be tampered with. A rigid orthodoxy can be as much an expression of an insecure faith as can radicalism. Secret doubts are erased not by working them through but by positively refusing to concede their existence. Orthodoxy, not Christ, becomes the rock of theological certitude. Blind faith, unwaveringly held, becomes a protective armor against the difficulties which time, history, and reason have thrown before the believer. Authority, not the redemption wrought by Christ, may come to be taken as the source of salvation; but it amounts to a salvation from danger, not a salvation of the self.

I have drawn exaggerated sketches here of the possibilities of self-deception open to the liberal and the conservative. It would be equally possible to draw a caricature of the "balanced" Catholic, one who tries to take the best from both the liberal and the conservative clusters of ideas and inclinations. For what could potentially be more dishonest than always and systematically refusing the challenges posed by the extremes of Catholic thought and attitudes? To deny that the complaints of the disillusioned rebel could possibly have weight, or that the anxieties of the rigidly orthodox about the corrosive force of false ideas could have a basis, to say, always,

[6] *Ibid.*, pp. 76–78.

that the "truth must lie somewhere in between"—could not this too become a courting of dishonesty, all the more persuasive because its great merit seems to be its sensible balance?

My point here is only to indicate that no position is, as such, immune from being put to dishonest uses. It is not possible to say that because a person is a liberal he is necessarily more honest with himself than the conservative; or that he is more honest because he is a conservative or a moderate. Similarly, there is no guarantee that the liberal will, as such, be a more honest spokesman for the Church in the public arena; or that the conservative will be more likely to tell the truth. All of these observations may seem obvious in the abstract. In the concrete they have an enormous importance. They mean that a person must never confuse the strength of his convictions with his ability to be honest. They mean that a person must never allow himself to believe that the holding of a position, whether liberal or conservative, obviates the possibility of dishonesty. Most crucially, they mean that honesty can be attributed only to persons and never to positions, doctrines, or to declarations of truth. Just as it is a linguistic misuse to say that "error has no rights," for only persons can have rights, it would be equally a misuse to talk of "honest doctrines." A doctrine can be, logically, true or false; only a person can be honest. It is, however, perfectly possible to speak of an "honest belief" or an "honest conviction"—as long as it is kept in mind that the word "honest" will refer to the way the belief or conviction is achieved and held, and not to the substantive content of the belief or conviction. One can hold a true position dishonestly, by proclaiming it true when one is not convinced that it is; or a false position honestly, by believing something which is not true.

CHAPTER FOUR

From Honesty to Integrity

By now I trust that my understanding of honesty has begun to appear in a somewhat clearer light. In an important sense, it is a concept which defies a dictionary definition; one can more easily circumscribe and characterize honesty than reduce its meaning to a set of clear terms. Nevertheless, it is useful to try to formulate a definition; this effort is made a shade easier when the context is that of Catholic life. Let me then offer the following as a reasonably close approximation:

1. In the public life of the Church, honesty will consist of a persistent effort to remove false appearances. This means that those in a position to present, explain, and defend the Church to those outside the Church *and* within it will scrupulously avoid doing or saying anything which makes the Church appear to be something which it is not. They will disavow distorted representations of the Church's doctrines, especially in claiming for them a clarity and unanimity of acceptance when these do not obtain. They will avoid overinflated rhetoric whose sole aim is that of embellishing the image of the Church and making misleading appeals to unregulated emotions. They will disavow those pious conventions which tend to strengthen the false idea that the Church is an abstract entity which has no essential contact with the

rough realities of human sin and finiteness. Public honesty will, moreover, entail the open recognition and admission of the existence of unresolved problems and dilemmas in the Church. They will not be concealed, nor will efforts be made to find ingenious ways of explaining them as "signs of growth," "healthy adjustments," "fruitful difficulties," unless there are solid reasons for doing so.

2. In the private life of the Catholic, honesty will consist of the total willingness of a person to admit to himself the reality of his human self and the actual state of his faith. This will mean, most importantly, that he will have the ability and the courage to confront and confess to himself any difficulties and doubts about his belief in God and in the Church. He will be sharply aware of any discrepancies between what he has been taught he must believe and what he does in fact believe. In addition, he will be able and willing to admit these discrepancies in public. Finally, private honesty will demand that the Catholic take all necessary steps to resolve any discrepancies he may discover—not by isolating his problems and ignoring them; not by grasping for easy solutions to them; not by willing them out of existence; not by leaning on others—but by daring to face them and to live with them regardless of the spiritual and mental stress they may cause.

In both public and private honesty, then, the ultimate aim will be to eliminate any trace of dualism. There must not be two Churches, one for public consumption and another for contemplation behind closed doors. There must not be two selves, one of bland, external conformity to law, custom, and authority, and one which is secret, known only to an individual himself. The Catholic must not be a performer, one who stages a public show in the name of the Church or a show within his private world for the sake of allaying his anxieties. The sociologist Erving Goffman has brilliantly characterized the nature of the performer:

> In their capacity as performers, individuals will be concerned with maintaining the impression that they are living up to the many standards by which they and their products are judged. Because these standards are so numerous and so pervasive, the individuals who are performers dwell more than we might think in a moral world. But, *qua* performers, individuals are concerned not with the moral issue of realizing these standards, but with the amoral issue of engineering a convincing impression that these standards are being realized. Our activity, then, is largely concerned with moral matters, but as performers we do not have a moral concern with them. As performers we are merchants of morality. Our day is given over to intimate contact with the goods we display and our minds are filled with intimate understandings of them; but it may well be that the more attention we give to these goods, then the more distant we feel from them and from those who are believing enough to buy them. To use a different imagery, the very obligation and profitability of appearing always in a steady moral light, of being a socialized character, forces one to be the sort of person who is practiced in the ways of the stage.[1]

Within the Church there are many motives for the practice of stagecraft, some of which have already been noted. What distinguishes the motives of the Catholic are undoubtedly the ultimate values he attributes (or believes he ought to attribute) to the standards to which he is committed. The good he represents is not just one more piece of merchandise but, rather, something which has as its main virtue ultimate truth. In the world of business such a claim is

[1] *The Presentation of Self in Everyday Life* (Garden City, N.Y.: Doubleday and Co., 1959), p. 251.

rarely made. The salesman will normally know that what he stands for has a limited value only. Yet unless he tells flat lies about the product he sells, no one will account it a moral failing if he spends most of his time trying to shape an image of it which will persuade people to think it better than the product of a competitor. It is taken for granted that he will exaggerate, that he will minimize, if not totally ignore, the merits of the competitor's wares. In his private life, the salesman will not be expected to convince himself that the product he peddles has an intrinsic merit which, in itself, precludes the possibility that anything better may be conceived. For the Catholic, such an approach to truth should have no place. Nonetheless, since he is normally aware that others will judge him partly in terms of his professed values, there are powerful forces operating to induce him to manage his public image in a careful way. The very firmness of his values makes them immediate prey to those who stand for different values. This assault, which may be more implicit than explicit in daily life, calls forth a variety of countermeasures: thus the door is opened for all the forms of dishonesty which are possible for the Catholic. His dishonesty becomes a way of defending his commitment before the probing eyes of the world as well as a way of defending his commitment to himself. That is why public and private dishonesty have a reciprocal relationship. And precisely because so much is at stake in Catholic belief it becomes all the harder to resist putting on performances. No one cares to appear in public with spots on his shirt and tie, nor does one usually care to think of oneself as full of uncertainties and contradictions. The good performer convinces himself that his act represents his true self; the more he tries to convince himself, however, the more he risks cutting himself off from reality. He becomes his mask.

Just why this kind of systematic self-deception is destructive of the self should be unnecessary to spell out.

The Difficulties of Achieving Honesty

Should we simply conclude with the advice: be honest? Should we say to those in a position to shape the public image of the Church: tell the truth? Should we say to ourselves: admit any doubts and perplexities? Of course we should. But in the end is not this very much like telling a person who enquires about the ethical life that he should "do good and avoid evil"? We have told him everything and, for just that reason, have told him nothing. He will at once see that everything depends upon what doing good and avoiding evil mean in specific situations. He will further realize that life presents comparatively few occasions in which the most important good stands out with unmistakable clarity. More often, his ethical choices will involve a weighing of comparative values; many goods will clamor for attention. The avoidance of evil may be the least of his problems.

An analogous problem arises in the quest for honesty, one by no means less complicated. Let us assume that one has determined to be honest. No more, he promises himself, will he present the Church in a false light. No more will he hide its deficiencies. No more will he have recourse to the rhetoric of evasion. No more will he avoid facing his own doubts. No more will he suppress his problems. No more will he try to convince himself that he is more secure in his faith than he actually is. Where does he go from there? In practice, he will almost certainly find that countless dilemmas stand before him. Take the matter of speaking honestly about the past history of the Church. What is the way of perfect honesty here? One possible course would be to state frankly that history displays many failures, and then to begin recounting these failures, amassing a sizable list of corruptions and sins. In the eyes of the critic of the Church such a performance could well be impressive: one will usually admire the courage of a person who is willing to display the skeletons in the family closet. In his own consciousness, the Catholic may undertake such a revelation with fear and trembling, and thus be able to feel that he has spared nothing in the way of candor—for it has cost him something. Yet at some point another question will arise: must he not also, in the name of honesty, admit that the past history of the Church has its bright pages as well as dark? Perfect honesty about the total record of history will necessitate giving credit where credit is due. This may seem an obvious point, but it is not obvious in the context of honesty. For are we to account as honest only that which is painful to tell or has not been revealed before? Is the only mode of genuine honesty that of a confession of guilt? It is very tempting to answer both questions in the affirmative. But if honesty is to have any meaning at all it must be compatible with the truth one knows, and to suppress one element of truth in favor of another is a dishonest procedure, however painful it may be to reveal the one element.

A failure to observe this rule accounts for the widespread misuse of the idea of honesty in the popular press. It has been common for some years now for publishers to advertise many books and articles on the strength of their purported honesty and candor. Yet not infrequently the basis for this claim is solely that the author takes an unpopular position, or discloses some well-hidden secret, or presents some cherished illusion in a new, less flattering way. It is as if the mere fact of departure from convention constitutes a guarantee of good faith. In some cases it very well may, but in the final analysis the degree of honesty which a work reveals will have little to do with the popularity or unpopularity of the views or revelations contained within it. Not everything that is called honest necessarily is. In the Church, just because there has been a considerable amount of dishonesty, it is all too easy to credit the man who says unpleasant things with a special degree of honesty. That criterion, however, provides no meaningful measure; at most, it is only an indication of the appearance of honesty. A man who, through ignorance, sustains popular myths may be more worthy of being called honest than one who, through an acute sensitivity to cant and hypocrisy, suppresses any deference to convention. Honesty can become as much a salable commodity as any other popular virtue, but amount to little more than a retailing of the sensational.

Still another dilemma will be posed by the conflicting demands of honesty and charity. In ordinary life, it will not always be a virtue to give such a priority to honesty that all consideration of the sensitivities of others can be brushed aside. One does not ordinarily (nor should one) tell a bumbling, incompetent child that he is bumbling and incompetent. One remains tactfully silent, doing one's best to help the child to improve. Nor does one tell an ugly woman she is ugly, or a man struggling with alcoholism that he is a disgusting drunkard, or an unhappy person that he is unpleasant to be near. All of these things may be perfectly true; but one important measure of human sensibility is the ability to restrain our impulse toward candor in favor of a richer response. It is not at all impossible, in fact, for honesty to be used as an instrument of aggression against another. What better way to hurt a person than to tell him bluntly what others think of him? or to recount with vivid directness his faults? or to refuse him any graceful means of saving face when he is in the wrong? Candor may be wholly on the side of the aggressor, but not charity. Within the province of the self, a like form of aggression is possible. The candid admission to oneself that one is a fraud, with principles unsupported by behavior, can easily shade off into neurotic masochism. In that case, honesty runs amok, seeking not the truth about the self but only its punishment.

It is not at all implausible to imagine that the current interest in honesty in the Church (not excluding this book) could, at least in part, be an expression of hostility toward the Church—a hostility whose main utility lies in its relative safeness. For the fact of the matter is that most of what is called "honest" in the Church today amounts to what is mainly critical of the Church. It is difficult for the Catholic in the contemporary world to avoid having some ambivalent feelings about the Church: faults are there to be seen, conflicts of conscience are there to be lived out in pain. But, as a Catholic, one cannot easily say one has mixed feelings about the Church, even though the real relationship of the individual to the Church may be a blend of love and resistance, just as it so often is in important human relationships. Yet if one cannot admit the resistance, what recourse is left? "Honesty" is left—that form of honesty, however, which is drawn to exposés, to brutal revelations, to battering human feelings (especially of those in authority) in the name of frankness and candor. The great advantage of honesty as a weapon of destruction is that no one can argue against it without at the same time seeming to approve deception. It is a perfect weapon for the unhappy Catholic.

One last difficulty may be mentioned, and here I will take the liberty of quoting from an earlier article on honesty:

One problem is that different kinds of self-deception (individual or communal) can come into play in different situations, calling, in turn, for different kinds of honesty. Thus the very fact that the Church's teaching on the immorality of contraceptives is a difficult teaching will mean that it will be just that much harder to be honest with oneself about it. The very fact that one might be willing to admit with all candor that it is difficult might, by the very same token, lead one to escapist doubts about the cogency of that position. Is it not likely that someone caught in a desperate conflict of family planning would be the most prone to believe that the Church's teaching *could* change? Or that it *must* be wrong? Or that it is all the fault of the celibate clergy? To go to the other extreme, would not the person who honestly believed the Church's position is irreformable be the one most likely to be dishonest about the kinds of difficulties which can arise (by shaping facts to fit doctrine)? It is as if, in each case, sheer honesty about one side of a problem paves the way for dishonesty about another.[2]

Honesty and the Elusive Self

My point in mentioning the various difficulties cited above is not to suggest that it is impossible to achieve honesty. I would only emphasize that it is no easier to be honest than to be virtuous, and that it is possible to commit as many crimes in the name of honesty as have been committed in the name of other goods. The honest criminal who readily confesses his crime is still a criminal. The honest brute who tells

[2] Daniel Callahan, "The Quest for Honesty," *The Commonweal*, LXXX (Apr. 24, 1964), 140.

everyone just what he thinks in no uncertain terms is all the more a brute because of his candor. Honesty can be used as a propaganda device (detailed horror stories have a special utility for the propagandist); as a means of self-aggrandizement (in a society which lionizes the scandalmonger); as a form of blackmail.

Most significantly, honesty can amount to nothing other than an expression of one's personal commitments. What will seem to be, at least to oneself, an instance of honesty can be solely a reflection of one's own stance toward the world, a function of what one takes to be important. For the reformer, honesty may mean a revelation of the failures of those bound to the old ways. For the adherents of those old ways, honesty may mean a revelation of the dangerous secular influences which he believes are shaping the viewpoint of the reformer. It hardly seems coincidental that so many calls for honesty are closely related to specific calls for substantive changes in doctrine and practice. The call for greater honesty about the marriage relationship coincides with a call for a re-evaluation of the Church's teaching on licit means of family planning. The call for greater honesty about the tyrannies of the Curia coincides with the movement toward collegiality in the Church. The call for greater frankness between clergy and laity, priests and bishops, coincides with a concern for greater clerical and lay freedom. This is not to say, in any of these cases, that greater honesty is not needed, or that the proposed changes are not of first importance; but it is to say that a desire for honesty rarely develops in a vacuum. Most commonly, it will only be a part of some larger spiritual or theological movement and will directly reflect the concerns of those intent on furthering the movement.

A point of still greater importance presents itself here.

Honesty is a relational concept, its practical meaning wholly determined by the context in which those faced with a choice of honesty or deceit find themselves. In the context of public honesty in the Church, the honesty of a person will depend entirely upon what he *believes* to be true about this or that point of Catholic history, doctrine, or practice. A person can be wrong and yet perfectly honest, just as he can be honestly naïve. That is why it is never possible to say with confidence that a person who distorts the truth is necessarily dishonest. Everything will depend upon whether he knowingly distorts it, and that of course is usually impossible to discern. Nor will it do to say that, because a person *ought* to know the truth, he is in effect dishonest because he has not taken the trouble to properly inform himself. It is necessary to emphasize that a person can be honest only about what he knows here and now. He may well be guilty of keeping himself in a state of ignorance, but in acting or speaking at any given moment on the basis of the knowledge he does in fact possess, he can be wholly honest. He will be dishonest if he acts or speaks on any other basis. In the long run, naturally, his honesty will have a far greater meaning if he takes the trouble to educate himself; to be honest and informed is more commendable than to be honest and ignorant. But there still remains an important difference between being honest about what one believes to be true and being informed; the norm for the former lies within the consciousness of the individual, the norm for the latter lies outside him.

A similar but far more complicated problem arises when one is faced with a choice of being honest or deceitful with oneself. The similarity is that, both when being honest with others about the Church and when being honest with oneself, it is necessary to measure honesty in terms of the knowledge possessed at a given moment. Just as it is possible to speak of possessing knowledge about the facts of Church life and doctrine, so also it is possible to speak of possessing knowledge of the self. The norm for honesty in both cases will then be one's frankness in admitting the facts at hand. But the analogy here can be misleading. As difficult as it often is to know which facts of the objective world (in this case the Church) are important and which are not, it is far more difficult to judge the relative importance of the facts one can discern about the self. What do we discover when we try to locate the "true" self? To take only that which is immediately available in our consciousness, we find anxieties, hopes, beliefs, emotions, perceptions of the external world, sensations of our somatic states, a fund of knowledge, a store of memories, desires, fantasies, and so forth. What we do not find is some single object we can label "the self," much less ready criteria by which we can distinguish a true, permanent self from its transitory appearances or manifestations. The permanent and the transitory are inextricably one. At most, we can discover connections: a recollection that our body is more or less the same body it always was; a chain of memories which connects our present to our past; a set of relatively steady dispositions to act in certain ways under certain conditions. The self is no one of these things by itself; the combination of all together constitutes its total makeup. If to the conscious elements one adds those inclinations, drives, and dispositions which hide in the unconscious, the self becomes that much more elusive.

What counts in this mélange? Specifically, if one wants to be honest with oneself, which part of the self is most important, that to which one owes the most attention? At the outset, it is apparent that one must make a choice, and this for the reason that the various components of the self are rarely consistent with each other. For example, our emotions may not be consistent with our aspirations, our rational conclusions may not be consistent with our ingrained predispositions, and our beliefs not consistent with our actions. If one is uniquely fortunate, and no inconsistencies are apparent, there may be no problem of choice. But few of us are so blessed: to talk, then, of being true to the whole self—and everything that makes it up—may not take us far. We can very rarely be true to everything at once. Hence we must choose, assigning priorities. This choice, however, will inevitably be influenced by our system of values. The philosophical hedonist may believe that priority should be assigned to his physiological drives for pleasure; for him they will represent the most important element of his selfhood. The rationalist, by contrast, may assign priority to his mental processes, letting their conclusions and directions be decisive. The romanticist may settle upon imagination and memory. The voluntarist will credit his will with supreme importance. To put the matter this way, however—as if people can easily make a choice and assign priorities—does not take us very far. No man is likely to be a pure rationalist, romanticist, or a pure anything else. To be honest about only one part of his self, even if he accounts it the most important part, might well lead him into dishonesty about another part.

An example may help to clarify this point. Let us imagine the case of a person who finds the doctrine of hell emotionally repellent, but who nevertheless accepts it as true because the authority of the Church, which he accepts, declares that it is true. Is such a man honest with himself? More than one answer is possible here: if, hypothetically, that man has decided that the states of his emotions are a better index to his true self than a docile acceptance of truths on the grounds of authoritative teaching, he would be dishonest to let the teaching of authority determine his position. One might well want to persuade him that his emotions are a poor norm for determining matters of this sort; but as long as that *is* his norm he will be honest with himself only insofar as he abides by it. If, on the contrary, he believes that his willingness to accept authoritative teachings should be the true criterion of his honesty, then he would be dishonest in allowing his emotions to determine his choice. In both cases, however, dishonesty is still possible. A man who accepted the doctrine of hell because of his acceptance of authority would be dishonest if he denied to himself the existence of a feeling of revulsion toward the doctrine. For that feeling is also part of his self; it exists and to deny it would be to lie.

That example is a relatively simple one. Since in actuality a given doctrine may bring into play a great many of the parts which make up the whole self, let us consider a more complicated situation. Imagine a person asking himself: Do I believe in the existence of hell? To discover the answer, he looks into himself. There he finds: (*a*) that he believes he ought to believe there is a hell; (*b*) that his reason is not convinced; (*c*) that his emotions are in revolt; (*d*) that he hopes there is no hell; (*e*) that he knows Christ said some things which seem to support the Church's doctrine and that he has no inclination to doubt anything he reads in Scripture; (*f*) that when the matter comes up in conversation he finds he is always disposed to change the subject and becomes almost physically uncomfortable; (*g*) that he remembers a time when the doctrine made perfectly good sense on all counts and caused him no emotional discomfort at all. I do not believe that such a combination of elements is at all impossible. But a combination of this kind will make it exceedingly difficult to know whether one honestly believes in the existence of hell or not. What will it mean for such a man to be honest with himself? It will mean being honest not only about one point but about all the points: he must be honest about his rational conclusions, honest about his emotions, honest about his hopes, honest about his knowledge, honest about his dispositions. Even so, he may still not honestly know what *he* believes: for the very word "he" suggests a unity of self which, on inspection, he may not be able to discover. And of course if he asks himself on another day the same question he may find that the different elements of the self have shifted in tone and urgency. If he has just finished reading in the papers of a particularly vicious crime, he may find that his emotions no longer revolt at the idea of a man being condemned to eternal damnation. But which day should count?

At this point, two conclusions appear inevitable. The first is that it is extremely difficult to be honest. The self rarely displays itself in an unmistakable way, with the priority of its components laid out in neat, hierarchical order. Choices must be made and the priorities established by the person himself who desires to be honest. It is no more possible for a person to examine his self from a neutral, value-free perspective than it is for the scientist just to explain the material world. In both cases, an order must be imposed. For the scientist, this order will come from his theoretical constructs, those heuristic devices he employs in order to make sense of the inchoate, unspeaking facts he sees when he observes empirical data. For the individual trying to discover a hierarchy of priorities in his self, a systematic order of procedure must also be brought to bear. He will find in the self only that which his intellectual and spiritual equipment enables him to find. The self will not deliver its priorities to him unaided. It will do so only if he imposes on the self an order of values. But once a person attempts to do this, he will appear to be caught in a vicious circle. For if he brings to the task of being honest about himself a set of values, how will he, in turn, be able to know whether he is being honest in establishing these values? He cannot measure them against the deliverances of the self; for the self will deliver to him only what the values inherent in his procedure enable it to deliver.

The Context of Honesty

This dilemma points toward a second conclusion. A quest for honesty will have no significance whatsoever if undertaken apart from a broader quest for a system of values, a means of establishing self-identity, and a search for personal integrity. This is the corollary of a point made earlier: just as a desire for honesty is unlikely to arise in a vacuum, so also honesty cannot be achieved in a vacuum. No greater mistake can be made than to believe that one can just "be honest." Inexorably, our honesty will reflect our values and our interests. That is why, as we found earlier, it is no mere coincidence that exhortations for honesty arise as a part of movements for reform. That is also why a disavowal of hypocrisy will normally accompany a repudiation of some substantive abuse which the reformer wants to see removed. A common goad to reform movements is the widespread existence of formal obeisance to old traditions coupled with an equally widespread bypassing of them in people's actual behavior. Hypocrisy will be inevitable when traditions have privately been rejected but where there do not yet exist the intellectual materials for the formation of an alternative system which will meet with official and public approval. During such moments of confusion (and many exist in the Church today), it will be necessary not only to look for the meaning of honesty but also for its uses. A failure to take account of the close interrelationship of honesty and ultimate commitments renders one liable, in the search for honesty, to succeed only in replacing one set of dishonesties with another.

Ultimately, any fruitful attempt to achieve honesty will have to be part of a larger effort to establish one's selfhood. A plan toward this latter end will have to be devised, of which an inspection of the self will form a part. Yet the devising of a plan will necessitate the establishment of standards, the development of procedures, and the fashioning of tools with which to make discriminating judgments. As soon as one undertakes these last tasks, one is asking: Who am I? What should I be? What can I make of myself? These are questions of identity and integrity.

For the Catholic, it is possible to be convinced of the worth of his faith, and of the various reasons offered to justify it. Yet he may also find it extremely difficult to establish an identity within that faith. It is easy to see how this can happen. The structure of his belief, at the level of intellect, has been given him by others. He is provided with an apologetic designed to show the credibility of the Church's claims. He has been exhorted to direct his will to desire those goods which the Church holds before him as worthy of his humanity. As likely as not, he has been suitably rewarded, by approval and acceptance, for showing docility. In terms of his personal identity, the important thing to be noted is that he has had no hand in creating the structure of Church doctrine and life which he is expected to accept. On the contrary, he must conform himself to the Church and not vice versa. In great part, as a consequence, his belief is something which has been superimposed upon his consciousness. This is, of course, the normal process by which a person is acculturated in any society: he is shaped by his elders and trained to accept the values which dominate their society. The first essential difference in the case of the Church is that the values in question are said to have a divine sanction and the society which inculcates them does so because of a direct mandate from God. The second is that he cannot achieve salvation merely by belonging to the group; he must personally appropriate its values.

While it is hoped and expected that the Catholic will, as he grows in maturity, come to make these values his own in a personal way—and not just because they are the values of the Christian community of which he is a part—at some point he will have to come to grips with the fact that he has been, almost unknowingly, conditioned and acculturated. Sooner or later, if he desires to establish his own identity, he will have to recognize that he had very little say in determining the content of those beliefs by which he shapes and directs his life. In a totally Catholic culture, an alternative choice may not present itself: no other possibilities of belief are available to him. But in contemporary society, where values compete with each other and almost any form of belief can obtain a hearing, the Catholic cannot escape noticing that in great part he is what he is because of his family, training, education, and religio-social conditioning. It is not just by chance that most Catholics come from Catholic families, any more than it is chance which accounts for Protestants emerging from Protestant families. On the sociological level, this is a trivial observation, of surprise to no one. But on the personal level, its recognition can come as a distinct shock, serving to shake any sense of self-confidence that one's religious beliefs are strictly a matter of rational judgment and choice. In an age which has become conscious of the power of social conditioning to create almost any kind of man imaginable, the shock can be all the more profound.

Another kind of shock is also possible in the contemporary Church. Those raised to believe in the inviolability of one of the many forms of Catholic life, or of one of the many modes of understanding the Church and doctrine, can find it extremely unsettling to discover that these forms and modes are in the process of being rejected or supplanted. It may not matter, in terms of a personal sense of spiritual security, that the changes have the highest authoritative sanction. What is crucial is that ingrained habits are being challenged, carefully nurtured rationales are being cast by the wayside, and strange new ideas and practices are taking the place of old ones. This can lead to a profound sense of disorientation, as if all the familiar landmarks on a beloved, well-traveled road are being obliterated by bright new symbols and direction signs. At such a juncture a person may well have no choice but to ask himself, as he may never have been forced to do earlier, just what it is that he believes, just what it is that the Church means to him. One part of him may grant that the Church has a perfect right to change; but another part may say that he simply does not know this new Church, that it is not the Church to which he has given assent over the years. Social psychology knows many parallel phenomena: from the anxiety which urban renewal can cause among those living in long-settled neighborhoods to the juvenile delinquency which can result from moving children accustomed to one

way of life into a milieu whose ways are different. That some
fundamental values remain intact in the new atmosphere will
not, in itself, ensure an easy transition. The Church is a mixture of timeless, essential values and accidental, dispensable
values; the changing of a large number of accidentals within
a relatively short time can be as distressing to many as
would be the changing of fundamentals.

There are, then, many ways in which a crisis of identity
can arise for the Catholic. In some cases, there may have been
no real identity in the first place, but only the passive acceptance of a set of beliefs and ways of behavior never integrated
into the whole personality. In others, an identity may have
been achieved, but one based on an overly rigid conception
of the Church and the intellectual and moral duties required
of the Catholic. In each instance, the equilibrium of the self
will hang by a delicate thread, subject to the ravages of cultural change, an exposure to different values, and the development of once dormant parts of the self. Flexibility will
be lacking, insight at a minimum, and anxiety attacks a constantly present danger. One might here define the ineffective
Catholic as a person whose Catholic identity is separate from
his secular identity; he may be faithful in obeying the minimal laws of the Church but give no evidence that his osten-
sible adherence to Christ has transformed his daily life. One
might be tempted to call such a person hypocritical, but it
would probably be more illuminating to think of him as a
person with a split self. One part is determined by the religious
influences in his life and the other by the influences of that
nonreligious society in which he lives his daily life. The two
parts of the self will have one thing in common: both will be
conformist. This split selfhood can afflict the Catholic who is
highly trained and intellectually sophisticated as much as one

with a humbler education and a more modest place on the ladder of worldly success.

Establishing a Personal Identity

Whether the drive to achieve a personal identity results from a shock to an insecure identity or from a natural growth in maturity, it is a drive which cannot be slighted. To do so is to lay the ground for a lifetime of self-evasions, to stunt spiritual growth, and to run the constant risk of living in a state of bad faith. To assume that the Catholic who is faithful to the teachings of the Church, who keeps the laws of the Church, and who does not entertain doubts must necessarily be in good faith would be a great mistake. If one understands the Church *only* as a source of authoritative pronouncements on the nature of truth and right conduct, such an assumption would make considerable sense. Good faith would then amount to perfect conformity, something which could be measured by "objective" tests.

But the result of such an understanding would be to reduce the meaning of the Church to the level of an authoritarian ideology, promising salvation to the individual on the condition that he efface his selfhood by an absolute commitment to externally imposed norms. It will not matter that the individual finds some of these norms unintelligible; he is assured that his difficulties have no real meaning as long as he faithfully conforms. Any such understanding of the Church is an abomination. Apart from its task of leading men to Christ, of providing the ground on which men can encounter the living God, the Church is nothing. The ultimate meaning of the Christian faith lies in the personal meeting of man and God. It is not commitment to a glorious idea or set of ideals,

as is characteristic of an ideology. It is not the kind of commitment which demands a communal solidarity solely because power in the world requires loyal men willing to sacri-
fice themselves for the good of the cause. Above all, it is not
the kind of commitment which excuses any sort of deception
and evasion as long as their purpose is a good one. To deceive
others for the good of the Church, to deceive oneself for the
sake of loyalty to the authority of the Church: each is still a
deception and cannot be covered by euphemisms. Though he
was speaking of the relationship of a person to secular society,
what Peter L. Berger has said of bad faith is pertinent here:
"We understand a man to be in bad faith who excuses himself by pointing to his social role and to the ideologies in
which that role is enveloped." [3]

With this point in mind, I want to propose a norm for
the establishment of a Catholic identity. The Catholic
should, as nearly as possible, develop the ability to discern the
difference between those values and concepts which have
been given to him by the Church and those which he has
achieved as a result of his own deliberate efforts. The result
of such an ability will be a clear awareness of all those forces
within the community of the Church which have led him to
his professed commitment to the Church. He will know the
part that fear of punishment, that parental and social education, that a desire for conformity, and that an unhealthy awe
of ecclesiastical authority have played. He will, that is, be
able to see how he has been conditioned to accept the values
which the Church and those Catholics with whom he has
come in contact have shaped his acceptance of the Church.
He will further have the ability to understand the self that he

[3] *The Precarious Vision* (Garden City, N.Y.: Doubleday and Co., 1961),
p. 89.

can observe by inspection: he will know why he is disposed to certain kinds of emotions in certain kinds of situations; why he follows one mode of reasoning in some circumstances rather than other modes; why he suspends judgment at some times but not at others; why, if such is the case, certain problems cause anxiety while others do not; and so on. That is to say, he will have the ability, in a manner of speaking, to stand outside himself and to discriminate among the various elements of the self.

To avoid any misunderstanding, I would point out that this ability would not entail any presumption that the acculturated self is necessarily a defective self; or that the self which has been achieved by deliberate efforts is in all particulars a superior self. For it may well be that a person has been conditioned and knows it, but that he has also by a free decision ratified the values given him. To be conditioned does not necessarily imply that one has been victimized; everything will depend upon the final judgment one passes on the means and ends of the conditioning. Moreover, one may well conclude that one's training did not curtail one's freedom—and thus was not coercive. Here I would only emphasize that the establishment of a self-identity requires that one be able to discover the difference between the conditioned self and the personally achieved self.

No less important is the ability to make discriminating observations about the achieved self. If the latter is the result of a personal appropriation of the truths of the tradition into which the Catholic is born, or the result of a personal effort to create meaningful ways of understanding what one takes to be the truth, then one must have the ability to distinguish the various emotions, inclinations and reasonings which went into its creation and which sustain its existence. One must know why one thinks what one does; why one feels the way one does; why one is apt to react in given ways. The achieved self will have its own dynamism just as does the conditioned self. That dynamism must be subject to inspection.

The Development of Integrity

The process of discernment and discrimination that I have suggested as a rough norm for the achievement of self-identity is, however, incomplete. Its drawback is that it is essentially passive, designed mainly to bring before a person the data which make up his selfhood. It will tell him nothing about what he ought to be, about the kind of self-hood he should be attempting to shape. It tells him in what his present identity consists, but not in what it ought to consist. In terms of self-honesty, it does not tell him what weight he ought to assign to the data revealed by inspection; it is a process of neutral inspection only. To gain a sense of personal integrity—a sense, that is, of wholeness of self, of a meaningful unity of the self—values must be assigned and their relative order determined. Specifically, this means that one must determine what value should be assigned to the various components of the Catholic tradition which have conditioned one; what value to one's own achievements in relating to this tradition; what value to one's independent insights into the nature of truth; and what value to the directions and guidance given by others. This assignment of values will constitute one step in the formation of a self with integrity.

A second step will consist in taking the necessary measures to see to it that the assigned values are honored in the practical working out of one's life, whether in terms of beliefs or in terms of action. That these values must be honored, if the aim of integrity is genuine, is inherent in their very establishment. For to establish a scale of values implies that they ought to be observed; otherwise their establishment has no meaning. The values are assigned as part of a dynamic movement toward wholeness. To complete this movement, and hence to take it seriously, means that practice must be shaped to conform with principle.

The importance of honesty in the movement toward integrity now stands out with a fresh starkness. Honesty is necessary in that examination of the self by which one perceives one's identity. Without it, there is no way of seeing the self as it actually exists. Honesty is equally necessary when values are being assigned to the parts of the self which are perceived. Values cannot be assigned arbitrarily, but only in utmost seriousness, with purpose and direction. Finally, honesty is vital when the attempt is made to put the values into practice; it will serve as one measure of how well this attempt is succeeding. How important, then, is honesty? In itself, honesty is an insufficient basis from which to shape the self, but it is impossible to undertake the larger task implicit in that shaping unless honesty is present. It has a place at the beginning, when the total data of the self are examined; a place at the mid-point when the self is being structured; and a place at the end when the structured self—or better, the self in the continuing process of being shaped—must be measured for progress and forward movement. This is no more than to say that honesty must never be absent.

CHAPTER FIVE

The Responsibility of the Church

So far I have argued that honesty, while indispensable, is by itself insufficient for the establishment of self-identity and for the shaping of those values by which a self with integrity is formed. While these latter tasks turn out to be of ultimate importance, it is not my purpose in this book to discuss them. They are problems of a properly philosophical and theological nature and there are ample resources within those disciplines for dealing with them. Yet since honesty is indispensable it is imperative to enquire further into the conditions under which it can flourish and develop. If, as suggested, the self cannot be seen in a steady light and directed properly without honesty, then it becomes vital to understand what is required to assist and encourage its exercise. I would propose that the problem is one of responsibility: on the one hand, the responsibility of the Church to make Catholic honesty possible; and, on the other, of the individual to be honest with himself. The present chapter will discuss the responsibility of the Church, thereby giving it a certain priority.

Why should the responsibility of the Church be given priority, when it might appear that honesty is peculiarly the duty of the individual? Here I would point again to the powerful role of the socio-religious conditioning of the in-

dividual in the Church. Ordinarily, the Catholic is introduced to the Church long before he is in a position to judge
its claims, to make a personal assimilation of its truth, and to
understand its nature. For years—probably until late adolescence in most cases—he will accept the teachings of the
Church without feeling the need to examine them with his
own reason. This is the way he accepts most values instilled
in him since childhood—the mores of his community, its style
of life, the local political values, and so forth. His acceptance
of religion will be no different, even though he may recognize its supreme importance (but that too he will have been
taught). The result of this formation will normally be a Catholicism well rooted in both his conscious and his unconscious life. To be sure, the degree to which the individual
actively works at his religion, lives up to its commandments,
and takes its claims seriously will vary from person to person.
Nonetheless, it will be a comparatively rare person raised as a
Catholic who will grow up wholly indifferent to the Church.
He will be respectful to the clergy, to the authority of the
Church and to the demands of the Church on his life. So
powerful is this process of assimilation that even an apostate
often finds he cannot get the Church completely out of his
system. There is thus a sense in which it can be said that the
Church shapes a person before he has a chance to shape himself. Before he is ready to ask himself who he is and where he
should be going he has already been given the religious context in which to find the detailed answers; and this context is
so deeply rooted in his personality that only the most vigorous efforts at adult independence will enable him to examine
it with psychological freedom.

The most important consequence of this strong hold of
the Church on the individual's mind and emotions is that the

Church has a serious duty not to misuse its great powers of education, persuasion, and spiritual coercion. Just as it is possible for a parent to shape a child in his own image, at the expense of the freedom of the child, it is equally possible for the Church to do much the same thing. The only forces which will naturally limit this power are those over which the Church has no control: the influence of the environment in which the person lives, the possibility of spontaneous rebellion, and the inability of the Church to control the individual every moment of his life. But even these important exceptions can be nullified by the sheer conditioning force of the tools at the Church's disposal. All of this means that the Church has a special responsibility to create those conditions under which honesty can develop and find expression. To expect that a person raised in an atmosphere where honesty was and remains impossible will come naturally to see its importance is to expect more than is likely. Put differently, there is little probability that a Catholic will be honest unless the Church has taught him how and has made psychological independence possible in the actual life of the Church.

Instruction by Example

Nothing is so persuasive as good example. With respect to honesty, the foremost way in which its value can be stressed to the Catholic is by showing it at every level of the Church's work and mission. The first level at which it must be displayed is that of the Church's teaching and disciplinary authority. Authority must, above all, be open in its motives, clear in its expressions, and direct in its conduct with those subject to its discipline. In Chapter 2, I sketched many of the actual and potential forms of public dishonesty. They should be repudiated: the pomp and ritual of ecclesiastical authority should never become a cloak for evasion; Church rhetoric should not be used to obfuscate or dissimulate; "higher interests" should not be evoked to justify deception. Of consummate importance, ecclesiastical authority should not adopt a public manner which is different from its private manner. The Church should not say to non-Catholics what it knows it could not get away with saying to Catholics themselves. A bishop should not say to his priests what he would not say to his fellow bishops; a priest should not say to laymen what he would not say to other priests; educated laymen should not say to the uneducated what they would not say to those on their own intellectual level. The only exceptions to these norms would be dictated by charity. There is always the obligation not to damage the personal good name of another, but this obligation does not encompass a ritualistic effort to cover up the incompetencies and mistakes of those in authority solely because they hold office. Nor does it encompass the indoctrination of Catholics with a notion of the dignity of office in the Church which blurs the distinction between the office and the person holding it.

There is in the Church something very akin to the practice in advertising of "image-building"; indeed, in the past few years, the expression has been freely used to characterize one task of the contemporary Catholic. It has been said that he must give thought to the non-Catholic's image of the Church: What do people think of the Church? What is their impression of the Catholic? While there is, no doubt, some germ of truth in the belief that the image of an institution is of considerable importance in a society where professed values and functions are not always easily conveyed, it remains a dangerous idea for the Catholic to work with. Its main danger is that it lays heavy emphasis upon appearance at the expense of reality, opening the way for hypocrisy, misleading claims, and an emphasis on accidentals rather than substance.

One implication here is that the Church, where it has not done so, must cease looking upon its ecumenical task as that of presenting a good "image" of the Church to those from whom it is separated. Some years ago, when it was seen that Christian unity would not come about by demands from "Rome" that Protestants and Orthodox "submit" to the authority of the Church, it was not at once clear what alternative stance could be taken which would be compatible with the Church's understanding of itself. Gradually a consensus developed that a docility to the promptings of the Holy Spirit, a recognition that He alone could bring about true unity, provided that alternative. At the same time, however, this crucial insight has often been slighted. The Church stopped talking (at least bluntly) the language of submission and ecclesiastical imperialism, but it did talk of renewing the Church in order that it might reveal to the non-Catholic where his true spiritual home lies. Thus a note of ecumenical pragmatism was introduced. In its cruder versions, much attention was paid to ways in which the Church could set about making itself look good to non-Catholics, assisted by a concerted campaign to explain and justify itself. Good works in the public arena—efforts toward racial justice, world peace, assistance to underdeveloped nations—would, of course, help the campaign along. In its subtler versions, the emphasis fell on the duty of the Catholic to show the world what the Church really is. Here there was less talk of "public image" and more weight given to the true Church as distinguished from the publicly visible Church. It was that hidden Church which Catholics had to show forth. (One is reminded here of the different strategies of an advertising campaign, one approach emphasizing a product's image, the other its intrinsic merits.)

The Church, however, is not a commodity to be pushed by better salesmanship. Any suggestion that it is will have damaging consequences. The non-Catholic will at once see through an emphasis on the polished face (even if it does, to some extent, impress him); he will remain (rightly) suspicious. For the Catholic the impact is much worse. He is being asked to help the team by putting on a good show: smile; be sincere; speak with conviction; not only be what the Church says a Catholic is but look the part of the image the Church is trying to convey. The whole priority of goods is wrong, and the perceptive person will see this. He knows, or ought to know, that he should only appear to be what he is—a man who, while striving toward God, has his feet still on the ground. He knows, too, that this is what the Church must appear to be—what it is. Anyone who tells him he ought to be something for the sake of pragmatic ends, however spiritual and good these ends, will become the enemy of his integrity. Sooner or later, he will become no less suspicious of the Church than the non-Catholic. He will see hypocrisy, and that because he is not being asked to *find* himself for the sake of God, but instead to *change* himself for the greater good of the institutional Church. To the extent that the Church stresses its public image, it will risk destroying its validity in the eyes of its members.

The Church must eliminate the discrepancy between its appearance and its reality. This can be done not by trying to change its appearance, but only by confessing and working to improve its human reality. Part of its whole reality is, of course, its divine origin and mandate. But no less a part is its humanity: its feet of clay, its failures, its sins, its omissions—and its efforts to put the best face on things. Appearance, in short, should disclose reality. The desire for a good appearance cannot be allowed to obscure what the concrete Church is. Nor can the exigencies of public appearance be allowed to dictate the Church's conception of its real nature—of divinity working through sinful humanity. There should be no hidden backstage in the Church, no secret place, that is, where the actors memorize their lines, fix their makeup and put on their costumes preparatory to appearing before an audience.

The world is the place where the Church plays out the drama of salvation; there is thus only one stage, and what goes on before the people must be the whole drama. Once this is taken for granted, there remains no place for pretense. What is seen would be all there is to see, removing the possibility that those outside the Church will suspect that much of what they observe has been fabricated for the sake of a good press. Perhaps it was part of the genius of the Church in the past to have been able to fabricate so well: its pomp and splendor, its worldly power, its exotic ritual were all capable of impressing even those most hostile to it. But in an age which works with a passion to see behind appearances, which is wise to the artifices of stagecraft, nothing less than full exposure will suffice. This is the age of the exposé, an age, indeed, where the very claim of innocence and purity is enough to make men suspicious. Make such a claim and at once the sharp-nosed ferrets will seek the dark corners, search out the cluttered basement, and check the attic for hidden skeletons. The impulse behind this is by no means always pure, but often it springs from the assumption, healthy enough in our day, that things are rarely what they seem. Woe to the one who tries to cover up: the downfall of a good man who does that is likely to be far more painful than that of a criminal who confesses at once.

But notice that in my last paragraph the pragmatic note was unobtrusively introduced: the Church must be an open stage so that the critic will not be able to expose it. That motive, essentially defensive, must be rejected also. The only motive worthy of the Church is that it may appear to be what it is: and it is a Church of struggling men more notable for their failure to follow Christ than for their success. Its glory rests solely on Him who is its source, its life, its end. Otherwise it is nothing. It is not, then, for those outside the Church that it must forsake sham, dissimulation, and pretense. It must be for the sake of the Church itself, that it may be true to Christ. Given this, all else will follow. The Church must be in harmony with itself. This it cannot be if it is forever adjusting its masks, if it does not come to a basic insight that too much of its life is a matter of front, and that the time for pretending has come to an end. It is not just the world which the Church has managed to mislead; it has misled itself as well.

A Sinful Church

But what are the deeper theological roots for this repudiation of an exaltation of appearance at the expense of reality? How, specifically, can authority convey to the Catholic the necessity for honesty? There would be no better way than to inculcate a living realization that the Church is a Church of sinners and a sinful Church. For here, in essence, is a theological truth which, if understood, would make it exceedingly difficult for the Catholic ever to think in terms of a pure Church undefiled by error and evil; a truth which emphasizes that the Church must always be a humble Church, a confessing Church.

But is it not an article of faith that the Church is holy? Of course it is, and a more important doctrine can hardly be imagined. Yet the holiness of the Church does not derive from the personal holiness of its members, nor from the goodness of its aspirations: the Church is holy because of its relationship to Christ, the ground and source of its faith. It is holy because of its animation by the Holy Spirit. Hans Küng has pointed out that:

> We must . . . remember that in the early period the attribute "holy" was used extremely seldom in reference to the Church and this, its original meaning, in no way referred to the holiness of its members but to the relation of the Church to God (holy in terms of "heavenly"), and above all to the Holy Spirit. Further, we must remember that the original question asked in Baptism, in conformity with apostolic tradition, was not merely formulated: "Do you believe in the Holy Church?" but asked precisely: "Do you believe in the Holy Spirit *within* the Holy Church for the resurrection of the body?" Because of the Holy Spirit the Church of men and sinners may be called holy.[1]

At the same time, it is necessary to keep in mind that the Church, as a communion, is made up of those who are the "called" (Eph. 4:1, 4), whose vocation is "to be saints" (Rom. 1:7) and "who have been sanctified in Christ Jesus" (I Cor. 1:2). Through Baptism, the Christian is at once initiated into the community and becomes a "new creature in Christ" (II Cor. 5:17). The people of this community are "God's building" (II Cor. 6:16), consecrated for God. In

[1] *Structures of the Church* (New York: Thomas Nelson & Sons, 1964), p. 26.

these respects also, then, those who constitute the Church can be called "holy." Yet, that said, sin is by no means excluded from the life of the individual, nor from the people together. Only in the very special sense that the Christian's vocation is holiness can he personally claim some relationship to actual holiness. To the point expressed by Hans Küng above, one must add a complementary note: "Whenever the holiness of the Church is mentioned today, we are prone to imagine a vague entity divorced from the reality of our everyday lives, a quality there but hidden in the real Church, at most visible in pope or hierarchy. Originally, however, *the holy Church* implied the real visible Church, the Church on earth; she was a Church composed of fallible mortals." [2] This same tendency to separate the real from the visible Church has led Josef Ratzinger to protest that "it is impossible to contemplate the Church independently of the men who make up the Church; the idealization of a Church divorced from the human element corresponds to no historical reality." [3] The Church is holy; the Church is sinful: both assertions are true.

Despite much polemic directed over the centuries against the belief of the some of the Protestant reformers that the invisible, spiritual Church is not the same as the visible, hierarchical Church, many elements of such a dichotomy can still be found in the writing and preaching of the Church. What is noteworthy about the Catholic version, however, is that all the values of the invisible Church are implicitly transferred to the visible Church. To make such a transfer plausible it is necessary to idealize that which is visible. That is precisely what is often done. One modern prelate talks of the

[2] "The Holy Church," in *The Church* (New York: P. J. Kenedy, 1963), p. 207.

[3] "Free Expression and Obedience in the Church," in *The Church*, p. 207.

Church's "resplendent and regal countenance," and a modern, much praised pope could say that "in regard to things temporal, she [the Church] is the source of benefits as manifold and great as if the chief end of her existence were to ensure the prospering of our earthly life." The trouble here is not that these assertions are false. But when they are put forth as the whole truth, they are misleading in the extreme; and such assertions are rarely uttered in any other way. They do not give any inkling that the Church is a Church of sinners and a sinful Church; they do not make clear that the Church has presented, and still presents, a countenance which is in many places a scandal. They do not make clear that the Church is not yet the kingdom of God come to its final term.

A Catholic who is raised and trained to take such a conception of the Church as the whole truth can hardly help being misled himself and misleading others. The probability is that such a person will approach the failures of the Church as only calling for excuses and evasions. Any failure on the part of the hierarchy, of the clergy, of the laity, will be dismissed on the grounds that these flaws do not represent the "real" Church. Every instance of sin, of injustice, of tyranny can be passed off as if it were only an accidental sore on the body of the Church, as an expression only of cultural forces, poor seminary training, bad catechetical formation, and so on. We may call this the tactic of the ready excuse; not surprisingly, it always leaves the Church in an impregnable position. Nothing that actually happens in the Church is ever allowed to count against it. Those who would take the Church to task can always be taxed themselves with a failure to understand the "essence" of the Church. But this is fraud.

Far better if those in authority in the Church, as well as

those in a position to provide instruction, continually make clear that sin is ever a part of the Church. I take that to be a primary responsibility at this point in history. Hugo Rahner displays great realism when he writes: "The Church, as she actually lives, suffers, and in many of her parts rots, is and remains also for us a test of faith—a trying, discouraging, burning anxiety. She can become a danger to faith, because we are all tempted to wish she would become more spiritual, more attractive, more impressive, more overwhelming—and then we begin again, even today, to play the ancient ghost game which drags on through all the centuries, from Montanus to Jansen and into the chambers of our hearts." [4] The "realism" of this passage lies, I believe, in Father Rahner's recognition that, despite all our bravado about the Church, it is for many just what he says, "a test of faith." For we have heard too little about the sinful Church; when we discover, from the fruit of experience, that it is sinful, we are all too ready to believe that we have made a dangerous discovery, one best put out of mind, best hidden from ourselves as well as others. What else can we do if we have never been taught about sin in the Church? In ignorance, there is no way of coping with an insight so threatening. In knowledge, however, we would discover that we are not alone.

Let me quote at length from an important article by Karl Rahner: "It is a teaching of faith that sinners belong to the Church," he writes, pointing to the Church's struggle against Montanism, Novatianism, Donatism, to the condemnations of the Albigensians, the Fraticelli, Wycliffe and Hus, the Protestant reformers, Jansenism, and the Synod of Pistoia. This applies not just to the ordinary sinner, the man who occasionally falls from God's grace; it applies as well to

[4] "The Church, God's Strength in Human Weakness," in *The Church*, p. 9.

the "man who really lacks the grace of God, who strays far from Him, whose destiny works itself out with fearful consequences to perdition. . . . He is not merely registered as it were in her parish files; he is a part of her, he is a small bit of the concrete embodiment of God's grace in the world, a member of the Body of Christ." [5] While Father Rahner goes on to show that the obdurate sinner does not belong to the Church in the same sense as those who possess the grace of the Holy Spirit (visible membership being distinguishable from fruitful membership), the conclusion remains the same: "The Church is sinful" and "one can no longer in any context of faith maintain that there are sinners 'in' the Church as in an external confessional organization, but that this carries no implication about the Church herself." [6] The "real" Church, the Church of full theological truth is not "an idea, an ideal, something which should be, a thing to which one can appeal from the concrete realities, something which can be approached merely but never quite realized." [7] On the contrary there is only one Church; and "she is the one Church that is and is to be believed, in all circumstances and at all times the visible and validly organized sum total of the baptized and in her external profession of belief, in submission to the Roman pontiff, one. Of such a Church one can hardly say that she has nothing to do with the sins of her members. . . . Thus the sin of her children is spot and stain even on the Mystical Body of Christ. The Church is a sinful Church: it is part of her creed and no mere conclusion from experience. And it is terrifying." [8]

[5] "The Church of Sinners," *Cross Currents,* I (Spring, 1951), 64.
[6] *Ibid.,* p. 68.
[7] *Ibid.*
[8] *Ibid.* Cf. E. Schillebeeckx, O.P., in *Christ the Sacrament of the Encounter with God* (New York: Sheed & Ward, 1963), p. 205: "The Church, as the

But Father Rahner draws from this a corollary which is perhaps even more terrifying, precisely because it strikes at that private sanctum of security in which the fearful Catholic feels safely protected: the supposed sinlessness of those in authority, at least while they are exercising their authority.

It is obvious that the sin [in the Church] exists not only in the private life of the churchman but can enter very essentially into the concrete context of his activities as a representative of the Church as well. When the Church acts, guides, decides (or omits to decide when a decision should be made), when she preaches . . . these activities do not occur by abstract principle nor through the Holy Spirit alone. Rather is this entire activity of the Church the activity of concrete men. And if these men are sinful, if they are shamefully narrow, sinfully self-centered, materialistic, sluggish, their sinful shortcomings will inevitably affect those actions which they perform in their capacity as churchmen and transact in the Church's name as concrete Church affairs.[9]

In saying these things, Father Rahner would by no means have us lose sight of the fact that sin, for all its prevalence, remains in contradiction to the meaning of the Church: "This Church in her concreteness is *the* Church, the unique Church, the Church of God and of his Christ, the homeland of our souls, the place where alone we find the living God of grace and of eternal salvation." [10] No less importantly—if we would be fully honest—we must recognize that we are all implicated in sin:

earthly sign of the triumph of Christ's grace, still remains in a state of weakness, needing to purge itself of all that is sinful. The fact shows us two things: first, that the glory of the Church on earth is a veiled glory . . . and second, and more especially, that the power of God is fulfilled in and through the weakness and poverty of the Church."

[9] "The Church of Sinners," p. 69.

[10] *Ibid.*, p. 71.

When sin in the Church calls up our own sin into consciousness, when it brings us clearly face to face with our own conni-
vance—whether we be priests or laymen, great or small in God's
kingdom—and the realization that it is our sins which are the sins
of the Church, that we have contributed our part of the Church's
poverty and plight . . . then we are in a healthy position to see
the sins of the Church in the right light. . . . We shall carry and
endure the disgrace of the Church as our own; she is in reality
ours because whether we will or no, we belong to her and have
sinned in her.[11]

Self-limiting Authority

While a full realization of the existence of sin in the
Church, and of the reality of a sinful Church, would do much
to thwart a temptation to dishonesty, further steps are necessary. I have already mentioned a truism of Catholic theology:
authority is service. On the face of it such an essential principle provides the firmest possible ground for a humble, self-
effacing exercise of office. It also makes clear that authority in
the Church can and must be distinguished from the rule of a
dictatorship. There can be no cult of personality, no deifica-
tion of the uses of power, no possibility of belief that a
man holds office solely on his own merits and subject to the
dominion of no one. In the Church, every man is subject to
God; that is why it is proper to say that Catholic authority is
always limited, always relative: limited by the sovereignty of
God, relative to the absolute dominion of God. At the same
time, God has given to popes and bishops the right to teach
and legislate in His name; their authority is thus binding as
long as it is properly exercised and does not demand of the

[11] *Ibid.*, p. 73.

Catholic what the divine and natural law prohibits. Still, it remains an office of service: to God and to that community which is the Church.

In the temporal reality of a Church embedded in time and history, a Church of men, it is, however, all too easy to lose sight of these important limitations of ecclesiastical authority. Though it is comparatively easy for a student of the subject to define the limitations, it would be rash to say that Catholics in general are imbued with a lively sense of their importance; one will normally learn of them, if at all, only in the later stages of a good theological education. The overwhelming emphasis in the Church is that of the rights of authority and the duties of those subject to it. Even the rich concept of authority as service, which ought to point up the humility necessary for authority, can subtly be used to engender the idea that those served are those who most need humility. How could anyone dare oppose an authority whose purpose is to serve one's ultimate good? How could anyone claim that he was the victim of tyranny when the exercise of authority was for his sake? To paraphrase Orwell: All men must be humble, but some must be more humble than others.

Along with their responsibility to inculcate a greater sense of the sinfulness of the Church, then, it should also be the task of those with the right to command to make clear their own limitations. A greater stress on the solemn requirement of the Catholic to follow the dictates of his own conscience, even against the Church and even though his conscience may be objectively erroneous, would be a help in this direction. It needs to be made more explicit that this doctrine applies as much to those within the Church as to those outside. There is no implication here that the Catholic should be taught to take authority lightly, or that conscience is not subject to authority, especially the authority of the Church; it is a question of balance and, at present, the common practice in education and preaching, in magisterial and episcopal pronouncements, is to say very little of the rights even of the erroneous conscience. A livelier awareness of those rights would make Catholics more prone to bring their difficulties before authority and thus, in the end, would give authority a better chance to respond and to lay its reasoning before those who are troubled by conflicts of conscience.

Those with authority can also do more to educate Catholics in its limitations by making far clearer the *possibility* that a given act of authority may not be the wisest or most prudent. The word "possibility" here is important. In exercising its authority the magisterium acts under the protection of the Holy Spirit, but this protection, except in the special circumstances of infallible pronouncements by the pope and in the infallible consensus of the entire episcopal body, does not guarantee that every individual act by a pope or a bishop will be a perfect act, not subject to the human knowledge and limitation of its author. In *Politics and Catholic Freedom,* Dr. Garry Wills poses the pertinent problem: "Since the gates of Hell cannot prevail against her, one can say that, in terms of a society's life and death, the Church is protected from the misstep that might be fatal. But can one proceed from this *infallibilis securitas* (as Cardinal Franzelin called it) to a judgment about the wisdom of any particular act?" [12] This question he answers with a persuasive No: "The Church's prudential infallibility guarantees the achievement of her essential aims; but, within this continuing *assistentia,* divine Providence commits the earthly government of the Church to its earthly rulers, men of varying capacities and

[12] Chicago, Ill.: Henry Regnery, 1964, p. 116.

experience." [13] "The attempt," he points out, "to deny or simplify this interaction of human and divine, of the eternal and the temporal, of good and evil affecting the Church's earthly history, has the most serious, yet the most unpredictable consequences." [14] For my purposes, the consequence of importance is that the believer may be led to think that those with authority are preserved in every particular from ordinary human biases and fallibilities. Thus is induced an awe of authority which effectively serves to maximize its impact and to minimize the creative and critical intelligence of the believer.

Father Yves Congar has spoken of a "mystique" of authority present in the contemporary Church, and whose roots can be traced to the sixteenth century. "This 'mystique,' " he writes, "may be characterized as the notion of a complete identification of God's will with the institutional form of authority. In the latter, it is God himself whose voice we hear and heed. The fairly wide margin which the Middle Ages still left for the subordinate's appraisal is for all practical purposes reduced almost to nothing. . . . the absolute standard of the divine authority has become, so it would seem, identified and invested in the human standard of the ecclesiastical authorities." [15] To the extent that this is still true— and one must note the great progress of late toward a reduction of absolutist thinking about Church authority—to the same extent does honesty become all but impossible. For if the Catholic believes that to dare a critical thought about the pronouncements and actions of authority is to directly chal-

[13] *Ibid.*, p. 117.
[14] *Ibid.*, p. 122.
[15] "The Historical Development of Authority," in *Problems of Authority*, ed. John Todd (Baltimore, Md.: Helicon Press, 1962), pp. 145–146.

lenge God Himself, then hardly any ground is left to voice honest difficulties and to exercise honest reasoning. How could one *ever* think that, in times of mental turmoil and uncertainty, one was anything but in the wrong?

It is the responsibility of those holding office to educate the Catholic to believe that his insights and his thoughts, even when they do not accord with those of authority, *may* be valid. It will remain the duty of the Catholic to presume in favor of authority—but this presumption should not negate the possibility that the dissenter *could* be right. To the extent that authority makes this clear, it will show forth its humility in an unmistakable way.

Authority can also display its humility by specifying very precisely the degree to which Catholics are bound by its acts. Dr. Wills has pointed out that one of Newman's important contributions was to show how a legitimate "minimism" of Catholic doctrine can contribute to an increase of faith in God and his love: "He fought the drift of Catholic sentiment into a view that faith grows by accretion of the things one can accept. As he says, intellectual honesty, belief in the ordinances of natural law, and trust in Providence, demand that we approach all truth with the critical standards of mature examination. To know perfectly what one must believe, one is obliged, also, to ascertain the points where he need *not* believe, or, even, *must not* believe." [16] But is it not unrealistic, because hopelessly impractical, to ask that authority go so far as to tell the Catholic what he need not believe every time authority has something to say? Or that it append to every pronouncement a guide to the degree of assent required? Of course it is. I am suggesting only that the Church educate the Catholic in these important distinctions and that

[16] *Politics and Catholic Freedom*, p. 228.

it reiterate them frequently enough to make certain of their living force. Needless to say, this education should begin at an early stage—before the Catholic has been so conditioned to the rights of authority that any possibility of effectively recognizing its limitations has been psychologically, even if not rationally, precluded.

In sum, I am suggesting that those with authority in the Church provide the Catholic with the theological and intellectual tools by which he can examine and evaluate what authority does. No one should have to turn to advanced theological works to discover that such tools are available; they should form an essential part of his initial theological grasp of the Church. It is a rare secular power which goes out of its way to give those subject to it a thorough grounding in its own limitations. This will normally be done by its critics, those who reject the authority or who want to see it harnessed in some way. But a magnanimous, humble, and candid authority will do this work itself. There will be nothing the critic can legitimately say which has not already been said—and propagated—by authority itself. Is this to expect too much, just as it is normally too much to expect of secular rulers? Why should it be, especially if the Church takes seriously its own teaching that authority is meant to serve God and does not exist for the arbitrary consolidation of power? The mark of the totalitarian political regime is that it does everything possible to enhance its prestige, seeking not to define it own limits but continually to extend them. It wants blind obedience; it wants the personal magnetism of the leader to obliterate any critical powers in the follower; it wants those led to be as putty in its hands. The Church in principle wants none of these things, but if it is not careful—if it does not go out of its way to counteract the herd instinct in man—

it will get them. Precisely because there is so much genuine and well-founded respect for authority it becomes all the more necessary that authority take care that this respect does not degenerate into a set of attitudes unworthy of the Christian belief in the dignity of man.

Bishop John J. Wright has put well the duty of the Church toward the conscience of the Catholic:

> Mindful that conscience can, while still claiming the name of conscience, be lulled, anesthetized, even deadened, the Church has the duty to seek the development in all her children of a moral sensitivity so acute that conscience would not merely react negatively to deviation from Christian perfection, but impel positively toward personal perfection, social reform and the building of the kingdom of God. Greater appreciation of this latter office of the Church in the formation of conscience would offset the temptation to pretend that the claims of authority to obedience have so stifled the initiative and freedom of devout consciences as to diminish the effectiveness of the Gospel and the Church.[17]

If this important observation holds true for the Christian's response to social problems in the world, would it not also hold true for his response to moral failure within the Church? To go a step further, should not the Church develop within the person a conscience trained and able to know when authority within the Church does not fulfill its own mandate? To train the Christian conscience only to know how the world is to be judged is to train only part of the conscience. The Church, too, can fail—not in its ultimate mission, but certainly in its concrete response to concrete needs. The standards by which the Church should be judged

[17] "Reflections on Conscience and Authority," *The Critic*, XXII (Apr.-May, 1964), 22.

are those of the Church; it is the Church which should provide them.

Practical Demonstrations

There are many ways in which authority can demonstrate its willingness to let its acts be judged. The most direct way is by encouraging the people (clerical and lay) to express their opinions, asking them to hide nothing, to fear nothing, to run the risk of rebuff. This is what Pope Pius XII came near to doing when he talked of the value of public opinion in the Church. This is what numerous bishops have approached in asking the faithful to make known their wishes about the work of the Second Vatican Council. This is what Richard Cardinal Cushing did in his 1963 Pastoral Letter, *The Church and Public Opinion.* "Some temperaments among those in authority," he wrote, "are inclined to narrow down the area of legitimate discussion, but this will have its own share of serious dangers. The formation of public opinion may be delayed by such action, but only for a short while. If it is long suppressed perilous frustrations will result, as well as an underground circulation of views which should have public discussion and exchange. Far better to tolerate some small indiscretion in the expression of public opinion than to discourage legitimate views and deprive the Church of that leaven which must invigorate the whole body." [18] Here is authority pointing out its own potential weaknesses; and here too is authority describing the antidote to them.

The most powerful demonstration of the ability of authority to empty itself of any desire to overextend its limits

[18] Boston, Mass.: Daughters of St. Paul, 1963, p. 16.

will be the existence of public opinion, freedom, and diversity in the Church. It is perfectly possible for authority to demand silence, and the Catholic spirit of obedience will normally make it likely that the demand will be honored. But this exercise of authority will show only the coercive side of authority; it will show only that authority has power. The permissive side of authority, which is slow to cut off debate, slow to impose silence, slow to censure one side or another in a dispute, will show that authority can restrain itself. There can be no open discussion in the Church if there is a constant worry that authority is hovering overhead, ever ready to pounce upon those who say what they think. Diversity in the Church will be a sign of this restraint. In the ordinary course of human reasoning—particularly speculation on a mystery as profound as that of Christ and the Church—diversity will be the natural result. If it is lacking, there is a good *prima facie* case that the hand of authority lies too heavy.

Yet a merely permissive magisterium is hardly adequate. Authority should direct, exhort, and inspire; it should be and it is, properly speaking, a source of the unity of the Church. But can it not also guide by its openness to suggestions, its willingness to listen to those who feel it may need rebuking, its encouragement of experiments and fresh speculations? In these cases it animates the community by showing its belief that the Holy Spirit works in the whole Church and not just in the hierarchy. By listening to those who believe authority must at times be fraternally rebuked it shows that it recognizes its possibility of failure in particular situations. By its openness to suggestions it shows that it does not claim a monopoly of wisdom. By its encouragement of experiments and speculations it shows its desire to learn and grow. It shows, in other words, that it recognizes itself to be a vessel of clay. The most imposing aspect of authority in the Church is that it has the protection of the Holy Spirit; and precisely there lies the most important reason why it can be open. If authority had to depend only on its own human wisdom, only on its ability to command human respect and awe, then there would be good reason for it to close in on itself: that is what authority inevitably does in the totalitarian state. But authority in the Church has no need to feel insecure. The stifling of freedom necessary for the maintenance of totalitarian governments is not necessary for the Church. Fear breeds dishonesty, and the suppression of liberty corrodes and falsifies the faith of the Church.

Guarantees of Freedom

Fortunately it is possible to say that the Church has already entered into a new era. What has just been said about authority in the Church merely echoes what many others have said; and one can find many practical demonstrations in the Church today of a new openness on the part of those in office. Nonetheless, the Church still has some distance to go in this direction. There still do not exist, for instance, sufficient guarantees of legitimate freedom in the Church: too much seems to depend upon the personalities of particular bishops and popes. What is permissible in one diocese may not be permissible in another. What may draw censure from one bishop may be praised by another. The freedom of initiative possible in one place may be flatly forbidden in another. The rights of authority in the Church have been well structured, and that is one reason why such variation is possible. But there has been no corresponding structure created to ensure the rights of those subject to authority. There do not

exist established means by which the laity can communicate
their views to the hierarchy. There do not exist established
ways in which the laity can air grievances about their parish
or organizational life, about the conduct of their bishops and
about the activities and directives of the Roman congrega-
tions. While grievance procedures exist for the clergy, they
are often ignored in practice, cumbersome in their operation,
and ill-designed to deal with complaints in an orderly, juridical fashion. The creation of an effective system of rights
and safeguards for the individual in the Church, whether
clergy or laity, would be a dramatic step on the part of authority to establish clearly its sense of limitation. An effective
apparatus for the solicitation of clerical and lay opinion
would demonstrate authority's conviction that good will on
its part is not a sufficient method to ensure legitimate freedom. It is not enough to say that those subject to authority
have inherent rights and potential contributions to make;
this must be shown in practice by the concrete initiatives
taken by authority to structure these rights and formally
elicit the contributions. Only then will honesty have juridical
safeguards.

The existence of a considerable amount of secrecy in the
Church stands as a sign of an authority jealous of its preroga-
tives and cautious about exposing itself to comment and judgment. Where matters of conscience are concerned, or the
safeguarding of individual rights to privacy, secrecy may be
justified. But the hiding, for instance, of financial matters—
whether in the parish or in the Holy See—has little discernible justification. The implication of this secrecy is that the
Church belongs to authority, as if it were a closed family
corporation whose books can be concealed from the public.
But if the Church is, as frequently proclaimed today, a com-

munity, then the Church belongs to the people as well as to authority. At the very least the former have the right to information: they should know how money is spent and how financial decisions are reached. One does not ask here that this information necessarily be available to the whole world, but only that it be accessible to the members of that community which is the Church. Nor am I suggesting that authority should give up its right to control the spending of money; that is not necessary. I am only urging greater visibility: the Catholic ought to be able to see the inner workings of the machinery of finance in the Church.

A secrecy about money is only the most palpable sign of more subtle forms of secrecy. It is often extremely difficult to discover why doctrinal and disciplinary decisions are made. Part of the difficulty stems from the relative inaccessibility of the probing work of theologians. In many ways this is inevitable since much of this work goes on in technical theological journals; anyone who takes the trouble, however, can get hold of them. What is not so inevitable is a tendency among many theologians deliberately to keep their speculations from the public eye, to deal with delicate matters of doctrinal development and change in the safe confines of professional preserves. The motive for this concealment appears to be a mixture of self-protection on the part of the theologians— presumably out of a fear that the magisterium will tolerate bold thinking in the Church so long as it is not made public— and of a wariness that the public will seize on tentative suggestions and explorations as an excuse to set aside established teachings. The latter motive has somewhat more validity than the former; it would be naïve to deny that public opinion in the Church could degenerate into competing propaganda campaigns making a crude use of the carefully nuanced work of scattered theologians. That is a legitimate enough consideration for a theologian. It would not be legitimate, however, for him to presume that the public never had any right to know of his speculations, as if this were a matter solely between him and the magisterium. Once again, it is a question of service to the Church. Is the work of the theologian designed only to serve authority or is it to serve the whole Church? It is only a small step from the former alternative to assert that authority has no obligation to make known the reasons for its decisions, a common enough belief of many theologians. One more step can produce the belief that it is not necessary for the believer to know the reasoning behind the teachings of authority.[19] The possibilities of dishonesty here scarcely need underlining.

There is no need further to belabor these points. The structure of the Church is hierarchical: authority proceeds from the top down and not from the bottom up. So far as this structure is concerned, it is crucial that authority itself undertake the task of creating an atmosphere which elicits and supports honesty. For the main obstacle to honesty between authority and the people is that authority has exclusive control over power in the Church. In principle, this makes it dangerous for the people to be honest: they run the risk of censure, hostility, or rebuff. There are no safeguards available to protect them should they choose to speak openly to authority. There exists no canonical obligation that authority listen

---

[19] Speaking on the Church's condemnation of mechanical means of contraception, for instance, two distinguished moralists stated that "the Catholic, therefore, must internally accept this doctrine as true and must externally conform to it. . . . And for Catholic living this internal conviction and external conformity is enough; it is not necessary to know why the Church teaches that contraception is immoral." John C. Ford, S.J., and Gerald Kelly, S.J., *Contemporary Moral Theology*, Vol. II: *"Marriage Questions"* (Westminster, Md.: Newman Press, 1963), p. 279.

to the people. There is little to curtail authority from punishing those who say what is on their mind. I am, let it be said, putting the matter in as harsh a light as possible. In practice, there is enough mutual affection between authority and the people to mitigate the theoretical dangers. Even so, an imbalance of power prevails, and the very existence of potential danger works toward suppression of direct speech. Because also of the respect for authority bred into the Catholic, it is far more difficult to risk openness than to remain timidly silent. For all these reasons, it is of the utmost importance for authority to realize that it must act in such a way that the imbalance of power in its favor does not turn out to hinder its mission. It must realize that excessive respect on the part of its subjects can lead them to hide their thoughts and feelings. It must realize that great power can engender a proportionately great fear. It must realize, too, that fear can lead to the formation of underground movements and currents which actually subvert that authority.

An Open Authority

For its own sake, authority needs honesty in the Church. It cannot adequately govern if it does not have some awareness of what the people are thinking. Nor is awareness enough: authority also needs to have a sense of the emotional tenor of that thinking. It must know how people feel and how they respond. If the people hide their secret self from authority, everyone loses: authority loses because it cannot speak to the hidden self; and the self loses because it becomes cut off from a vital source of illumination. There are many things authority needs to know: Are the teachings of the Church being understood? Is a clarification of this or

that point of doctrine necessary? Do the people have problems different from the commonly publicized ones? Have
social changes made the observance of particular prescriptions of Church law more difficult than was once the case?
Are there some valuable new viewpoints circulating through
the Church which would be worth assisting? Are there some
dangerous trends gaining ground which are weakening Catholic vitality? A bishop or a pope who does not ask questions of this kind, and who does not provide the conditions which enable the people to give frank answers, can easily come to live in a world of illusion, cut off from reality,
exposed only to myths and deceptions. The structure of authority will remain intact, but its substance will have been
gravely weakened. Only an authority willing to expose itself
—to hear of the existence of complicated problems, to hear
unpleasant things said, to hear how and where the people
have believed it to fail, to hear of its own shortcomings—only
this kind of authority can have full confidence that it has
done all in its power to get at the truth. Only an authority
which creates safeguards for those who would be honest, creates rights for those who believe they have grievances, and
creates formal means of ensuring a full airing of opinions and
suggestions can be certain that it has done everything possible to preclude the sense of apprehension, caution, and circumspection which are the marks of those subject to authoritarian regimes in the political sphere.

Yet it is not enough to say that only authority needs
greater honesty from the people. The people themselves need
it. The twentieth century has brought forth a whole host of
new crises, some challenging, some threatening, for the Catholic. Every age has posed threats to Christian faith; that is nothing new. But our age seems to be different. In the past, at least

in the West, Christianity reigned supreme. Any challenges to this supremacy came from minority forces: from de-Christianized thinkers and political leaders; from ideological movements whose power stemmed more from the dedication of their proponents than from the massed outburst of the ordinary man; from intellectual currents whose origins could be traced to a relatively few seminal figures. If it was the nineteenth century which sowed the seeds of the twentieth—in the advent of depth psychology, behaviorism, nihilism, totalitarianism, social messianism—the seeds have now ripened. At one time, not very long ago, the Church could cope with these forces by sending an elite corps of theologians and philosophers into the fray: few lay people and priests had an education sufficient to make sense of the trends themselves, and fewer still could have any idea of the intellectual roots which helped to sustain them. Thus in one way it was necessary for the Catholic to defer to the professionals in the Church; he had no choice but to hold fast to the faith and let those specially trained find answers for him.

No such easy solution is possible today. Mass education and the power of modern communications enable the Catholic to have a good idea of the world in which he lives. The time lag between the emergence of new intellectual currents and their passage into the mainstream of popular culture is startlingly short. The power of new ways of thinking to send an immediate shock wave through society is palpable today. The possibilities of popularizing and publicizing new scientific discoveries, new psychological theories, new systems of ethical thinking, new ways of explaining human conduct are almost unlimited. There is no practical way in which the Church, even if it wanted to, can quarantine the Catholic from these things: they are part of the air he breathes. The

most important result is that the individual Catholic can no
longer afford the comfortable solutions of the past. He cannot
turn over his intellectual and theological problems *en bloc* to
specialists. He cannot wait while the theologians work out
complicated contemporary puzzles at the slow pace necessary
to do it properly. He cannot always defer to the theologians
—for they may be no clearer about the nature of some fresh
complexity than he is. Nor can he wait for the magisterium
to speak, since it in turn will await the work of the theologians. No matter how hard it might try, the magisterium is
unlikely to be able to speak quickly and clearly to contemporary problems as fast as they now arise. Even when it does
speak, more time still will be needed for its guidance and
insight to take root. Inevitably, the Catholic is being thrown
more and more on his own resources, even when he is
fully willing to respect the Church's judgment. For him to
wait patiently for guidance, to suspend all judgment, to defer
all decisions, to put hard questions out of his mind until he
has been told what to think—these time-honored stratagems
of the confused Catholic will sustain him no longer. Above
all, he cannot pretend to himself that no problems exist or
that, if he just bides his time, everything will work out for the
best.

What the contemporary Catholic most needs is an atmosphere in the Church which enables him to bring his confu-
sions and uncertainties into the open. He cannot, in our age,
escape perplexity; at the same time, he cannot keep his con-
fusions bottled up within him. Should he try to evade difficulties, or segregate them to some private corner of his mind,
they will take their toll: in personal irresponsibility, in a
faith hiding cancerous sores, in an identity which has not
come to terms with itself. Should the teaching authority of

the Church, or those with pastoral responsibility, give him the impression that his doubts and his questions may be dangerous if made public, then he will truly be trapped within himself. Should he come to believe that the existence within him of intense worries about doctrines of the faith will be taken as a sign of rebellion and pride if he confesses them openly, then he will be doomed to suffer unaided. An authority which conveys the impression that it wants to hear only from the serene Catholic, the secure Catholic, the Catholic of untroubled faith, hurts not only itself but even more can do lasting damage to those about whom it should be most concerned.

To relegate the perplexed Catholic to the secrecy of the confessional, as if his problems were uniquely uncommon and to be solved only by private counsel and fervent prayers, is to do nothing less then to cut him off from the community of the Church. In another time, it might have been possible to assume that the perplexed Catholic was, almost by definition, a special, rather odd person. In our day, it will be a rare Catholic who is not troubled in one way or another. Some are bothered by the seeming inability of the Church to adapt itself to its own contemporary needs. Others find that the traditional language of the Church means little to them; it is not so much that they reject the Church's teaching, but rather that, phrased in an idiom of centuries long past, it conveys no significant meaning. Others are anguished by the failure of the Church to be a decisive moral force in the world. Not a few, by contrast, find the trends inspired by the Second Vatican Council disturbing; for them, the Fathers seem bent on renewing the Church beyond recognition. Their anguish also counts.

In recent years it has been persuasively argued that the

Church is a community and not a set of discrete individuals working out their salvation side by side. But if this is so—if the Church is the "people of God"—then the Church should be a place where men can suffer together as well as rejoice. No Catholic who finds his faith wavering, his commitment uncertain, his sense of meaningfulness as a Christian confused, should be forced to retreat within himself. The Church, and especially the teaching authority of the Church, should want to hear of his pain. His fellow Christians should want to hear of it. A brother is afflicted—we must all bear his affliction: that is how the Christian should respond. A brother is tormented by doubt—but, then, do we not all have to face this at some time during our life, perhaps often? We are all bound together in the Lord; but are we not bound too in the uncertainty which life in the modern world forces upon us? To place the doubter or the perplexed of spirit automatically under a cloud of suspicion, to ask him to keep his problems to himself lest he infect the whole people, to demand of him silence when he most needs to share his difficulties—these are the marks not of a true community but of a power structure intent on preserving itself from suffering. What is the responsibility of the Church? To make honesty possible so that no Catholic is forced to leave the Church before the Church has suffered with him. To make honesty possible so that no Catholic will have to retreat within himself while maintaining a façade of blissful certainty. To make honesty possible so that nothing is hidden from authority, and no illusions can gain ground.

CHAPTER SIX

The Responsibility of the Individual

A<small>T</small> the beginning of Chapter 4 I characterized private honesty as the total willingness of the Catholic to admit the reality of his self, particularly where it comes to bear on the difference between what he thinks he ought to believe and what he does in fact believe. At the same time, I suggested that honesty cannot be static, but must instead be dynamic, continually present in the attempt to discern one's identity and in the larger task of shaping an integral self. There is, however, something forbiddingly abstract about assertions of that kind. Why, after all, should one take the trouble to be honest and the equally hard steps necessary to shape the self? St. Paul says of Christians that their love "bears with all things, believes all things, hopes all things, endures all things" (I Cor. 13:7). We also have Christ's injunction to be as little children. Do not passages like these seem to militate against the tortuous self-analysis needed to achieve honesty, identity, and integrity? Commitment to Christ should bring joy and peace. But how can it if we never let ourselves alone, if we never cease probing our reason, emotions, and inclinations? The figure of the Catholic rustic is an appealing one: a simple Christian, secure in his faith, constant in his piety, steadfast and unfeigned in his loyalty, untroubled in mind and heart. It is an image almost overwhelming in its purity, a reproach to those whose vision is clouded, whose inner life is jagged, whose dedication is beset by uncertainty and turmoil.

But images are not reality. If Christ promised us peace, he did not promise that the way to peace would be easy. His Word of salvation, the Good News of His life, death, and resurrection was not a magic exemption from pain and travail. Christ promised us redemption, bearing witness to this redemption by the glory of Easter. But He also showed us, by His agony in the garden, the price we have to pay to share in His glory. Christ does not fit the image of the rustic Catholic. He did not accept the chalice of crucifixion with equanimity. Had not the Father willed otherwise He would have let it pass. Think, too, of St. Thérèse of Lisieux. Here is a saint proclaimed as a model of childlike peace and fidelity, a saint whom early hagiographers presented as the very prototype of Christian simplicity. But what do we discover when we look more closely, when we see real pictures of her and not those false ones at first circulated by her order and her admirers? We find a saint in agony, a woman who is not a child, tormented at the end of her life by an almost overwhelming sense of emptiness, hanging on to God in the midst of a relentless aridity of mind and emotion. "Lord, I believe; help thou my unbelief"—if one is looking for an image, these words evoke one which is at the very center of the reality of Christian life.

If we now ask again the question—"Why take the trouble to be honest? "—an answer is at hand. We cannot, for one thing, long survive in a world of illusion which purports to be Christian. The actual reality of our Christian life will be one of struggle and turmoil. Christ promised that the Holy Spirit would protect and guide the Church; but He did not promise a Church which would solve all our problems for us. Nor did he promise a Church which would be totally free of stupidity, shortsightedness, irresponsible uses of power, passing failures, and grievous moral faults. In our inner life, where we are constantly forced to grapple with complex intellectual and moral dilemmas, we can expect no respite from perplexity, even when we have Christ and the Church as a ground on which to stand. The Church will help us with our perplexity, but it cannot banish it. So, too, the Church can tell us in a general way who we are and what we should be. But it cannot climb into our minds and emotions and actively shape the person we should become. We can only do that ourselves, taking from the Church what it has to give, but knowing that in the end we are on our own. No one can bear our suffering for us, nor can anyone make our decisions for us. To lean upon the authority of the Church, by way of defaulting on our own responsibility to think and choose, is to run from our human dignity. To let others, whatever their stature or office, form our inner life is to abdicate our human freedom.

Christian Individuality

Honesty, then, is absolutely essential if we are to discover who we are, and to make that discovery an occasion for progress: progress toward the Lord, progress in the service of the Church, progress in the shaping of our own life and destiny. The distinctiveness of our individuality is the key here. The reason we cannot be content with conformity to the expectations of others—whether those of nation, friends, family, or Church—is that these expectations tell us little about who we are as specific persons. Each of us has his own history, his own private perspective on reality, his own set of problems and conflicts, his own mind, talents, and sensibility. It is illuminating to know I am, as a man, made in the image of God; but until I have discovered what this means for me as a distinct person—in *my* life, not in that of the human species—I know little more about myself than if it is pointed out that man is a featherless biped.

In terms of Christian faith, it is nothing less than a disaster to deny our individuality. To pretend to ourselves that our faith is serene, by resolutely refusing to face difficulties festering below the surface of our consciousness, is folly. We run at least the risk of losing contact with God: either by way of an accumulation of uncertainties which may one day suddenly overwhelm us, or by a gradual atrophy of our spiritual capacities. Nothing will be left but a shell, one which may well fool those around us, but which we will know to be empty. In terms of our service to the Church, the consequences can be no less disastrous. To pretend that we accept doctrinal formulations which mean nothing to us as individuals is to sustain only our craving for acceptance and security. Anyone can play the part of the brainwashed prisoner, repeating mechanically what his captors have told him is the truth. With some training, it is possible to become adept at manipulating the language of faith and doctrine, even when one has no personal idea what this language means. This too is the way to delusion. Just as fear of the Lord may be the beginning of wisdom, so too there is a sense in which conformity to the Church will aim us in the right direction. But if at some point—or better, continually—we do not question our conformity, we will be nothing as Christian individuals. Neither will it be possible to serve the Church. We will be living a life of sham.

It is all too tempting, however, for the Catholic to look upon his individuality as caught between two mutually exclusive goods. At one pole, there is the apparent good of perfect submission to the Church: docility to authority combined with conformity to the prevailing piety of the Catholic community. Individuality here is sublimated, the private dynamic of self transmuted into automatic identification with the collective whole. At the other pole is pure self-direction, a determination to sift everything, a refusal to accept any part of the collective whole. The dilemma is false, but its origin is easily understood in those instances where a person has been taught to believe that the Church is everything and he is nothing. If one takes this to be so, the only alternative to absolute submission which may seem available is absolute rejection of the Church; it becomes a black-and-white matter.

But the dilemma is false. In the first place, it is only as a unique individual that one can be a Christian. A faith which does not encompass a personal relationship with God, or at least a steadfast attempt to establish such a relationship, is not faith at all. There is a perfectly legitimate sense in which it is possible to say that a person could keep all the Church laws but still not have faith; one could, conceivably, refuse to burn incense to pagan gods, socially identify oneself with the Christian community to the ultimate extent of martyrdom, but still, for all that, not have faith. There is no *externally* "Christian" behavior incompatible with a total absence of a relationship with God. Above all, membership in the Church, even when accompanied by a perfect conformity to the laws and doctrines of the Church, does not mean that one is necessarily a Christian. Only one's personal relationship to God, one's living translation of Christianity into one's existential situation, can ensure that. "Not everyone who says to me, 'Lord, Lord,' shall enter the kingdom of heaven" (Matt. 7:21).

The dilemma is false, second, because even within the radius of docility to the Church there remains the absolute necessity of decision and responsibility. The demands of morality entail the application of general principles in concrete situations; that requires intelligence and prudence. Moreover, since moral decisions will have implications for others, one is never relieved of the responsibility of asking whether the principles are, as claimed, moral. A man would be as irresponsible in disclaiming any duties of judgment concerning principles as he would be concerning their application. The bureaucratic or totalitarian ethic says that one is responsible only for putting principles into practice. A Christian ethic worthy of the name will require that one raise moral questions about the ethic itself. Does it produce good fruits? Does it realize man's freedom and dignity? Does it manifest love? Similarly, an assent to Church doctrine carries with it a responsibility for understanding what one accepts. To say Yes to the words of doctrine while remaining wholly ignorant of their content signifies little; that is the mark of the child, not the adult.

A third reason the dilemma is false is that it assumes there can be a perfect overlap of individual and Church. Karl Rahner, addressing himself to the meaning of freedom in the Church, puts the fallacy of such reasoning in these terms:

Fundamentally all moral decisions which have to be made by the Christian—and all his decisions have a moral and Christian side to them—have also a concrete and individual dimension which of itself and directly cannot be covered at all by the authority of the Church. . . . This is a zone of freedom where the

Church leaves the individual Christian to himself, to his conscience and to the guidance of the Holy Spirit. . . . The ecclesiastical and the concrete ecclesiastical reality, on the one hand, and what is Christian and what is justified before God, the Creator of the universal *and* the individual, on the other hand, never coincide completely.[1]

Commenting on the same point in another place, he notes that "we cannot say this is accepted as a matter of course." [2] That is surely an understatement.

Charism in the Church

But more is at stake here than the preservation of a private sphere of freedom. The Church no less than the Christian needs this freedom. The Church needs it because, if the illumination of the individual which can be the gift of the Holy Spirit is to be of profit for the whole Church, the Church must be receptive to personal insight, holiness, and genius. In addition, the person himself will have the duty to let the stirring of the Holy Spirit within him be known to the Church. That he must also, at the same time, submit these stirrings to the judgment of the Church does not alter the matter. "True obedience," in the words of Father Josef Ratzinger, "is that which remains obedient even while bearing witness in suffering; it is that obedience which is forthright truthfulness and which is animated by the persistent power of love. . . . What the Church needs today, as always, are not adulators to extol the status quo, but men whose humility and obedience are no less than their passion for

---

[1] *Theological Investigations* (Baltimore, Md.: Helicon Press, 1963), II, p. 105.
[2] *Nature and Grace* (New York: Sheed & Ward, 1964), p. 27.

truth; men who, in a word, love the Church more than ease and the unruffled course of their personal destiny." [3]

There is in the Church a place for prophetic witness. The Old Testament prophets, it will be recalled, brought the witness of truth to bear on the pretensions of false religion: it was not "the world" they condemned but those who, in the name of God, were false to God. "Do not stifle the Spirit" (I Thess. 5:19) is a command to the Church of far-reaching importance. It is a recognition, to return again to Father Karl Rahner, that "the Spirit has always held sway anew in the Church, in ever new ways, always unexpectedly and creatively, and bestowed His gift of new life. He has never abolished official authority and laws, which after all derive from one and the same Spirit, but again and again brings them to fulfillment in ways other than those expected by the 'bureaucracy,' . . ." [4] This is the truth of charism: the gifts of the Holy Spirit are available to every member of the Church and not just to those who hold office. There is, naturally, always the possibility of false prophecy, of private delusion masking as the direct inspiration of the Holy Spirit. That is why, for the sensitive person, charism will always carry with it suffering. The discerning of the Spirit requires the most careful and painstaking examination, an interrogation of the self which leaves no stone unturned, no possibility of self-deceit unexplored.

Even when this has been done, the suffering may not be at an end. Opposition can normally be expected, "For it is painful to fulfill the task set by the charism, the gift received,

---

[3] "Free Expression and Obedience in the Church," in *The Church* (New York: P. J. Kenedy, 1963), p. 212.

[4] *The Dynamic Element in the Church* (New York: Herder & Herder, 1964), p. 58.

and at the same time within the one body to endure the opposition of another's activity which may in certain circumstances be equally justified. One's own gift is always limited and humbled by another's gift." [5] Both discernment and courage are required: discernment in judging oneself, courage once that judgment has, in humility, been soberly rendered. "We must also be able to have the courage (for this can be the precise function given by the Spirit to a particular member of the Church), to say No in the Church, to make a stand against certain trends and spirits, even before the official hierarchy itself has been alarmed. In fact, such a protest can be God's means of rousing his ministers to act." [6] The existence of charism thus provides the individual with a firm theological base for public honesty: not only will honesty be legitimate, but there can be circumstances in which public testimony will be his duty.

Yet it is not necessary to turn to the dramatic reality of charism to see how honesty can be of service to the Church. This might suggest, in a misleading way, that only under the most extraordinary circumstances could the individual dare to speak his mind in the Church. Often enough when the role of prophecy in the Church is discussed the examples given are those of a St. Francis, of a St. Paul withstanding St. Peter, of a St. Catherine of Siena. They are pertinent examples, but in their own way intimidating; few of us would care to presume the possession of the spiritual gifts and destiny of such great saints. In the ordinary course of events, however, it should not be necessary to evoke those exalted models. For one thing, it will be comparatively rare for the individual to find that his prophetic mission is to bring some new wisdom

[5] *Ibid.*, p. 77
[6] *Ibid.*

to the whole Church, or say, to rebuke a pope. A mission of that kind, if we take the concept of charism seriously, is certainly possible; but it will be something extraordinary. For another, the Church should rarely need such a radical illumination or chastisement. What it always needs is the more pedestrian intelligence, concern, and good will of its members. A pope will require the counsel of those in a position to advise him: to point out his missteps, to call his attention to pressing problems, to inform him of the undercurrents in the Church, of theological and social developments. A bishop will need such counsel as well, as will a religious superior, a pastor, and a priest. Few of us will be able to reach the ears of a pope, and not many more will be able to make their intelligence available to a bishop. But on the parish level, or in the life of obscure organizations, opportunities will increase. They should not be slighted, for it is as much on this hidden level —of a priest speaking to a pastor, of a nun to her superior, of a layman to a priest—as in the offices of popes and bishops that the vitality of the Church will be decided. Courage will be required here too, all the more so when there is no special training or reputation to commend an isolated person's insights. One might, in this respect, speak of an extraordinary charism and an ordinary charism. The former would pertain to those unique occasions when it falls to the individual to speak to the whole Church; the latter when it is a matter of applying the stirrings of the Holy Spirit within the very limited community of the parish, or the school, or the organization.

All of this is only another way of saying that everyone in the Church is responsible for the Church. This responsibility will be different for different people, according to their talents and gifts. But no one can claim he is without obligation to think of the good of the Church, or claim he has no duty to communicate his own observations and conclusions to those in the Church who might be able to make use of them. Those who hold office should be open to the wisdom of the least of those whom they command; but these latter, in turn, must present themselves to authority, not shirking the burden of informing them of what they think, see, and feel. This is especially important today, at a moment in history when the consciousness of modern man is being shaken to the core. In the preceding chapter it was suggested that authority needs to create those conditions under which honesty can flourish in the Church. Yet the individual member of the Church must do his part as well, running the risk of misunderstanding, rebuff, suspicion, and rejection. He must be honest even if, unhappily, authority shows no willingness to listen or seems to want only adulation and deferential silence. This seems to me a solemn duty of the Catholic, a duty best carried out in an atmosphere of mutual openness, but a duty even where that openness does not exist. St. Paul writes: "Let him who is instructed in the word share all good things with his teacher" (Gal. 6:6). There is no reason to assume that this exhortation applies only when the teacher has a taste for sharing.

The Duty of Judgment

It was also urged in the previous chapter that authority should equip the individual to assess its actions. This will not mean that the individual can pass judgment according to standards which are incompatible with Christianity; there can be no appeal to alien norms. It means, instead, that authority in the Church, as the Church itself teaches, is always subject to the sovereignty of God. When those who rule abuse their power, when they cease to serve, they stand already under the judgment of God. Authority cannot command obedience to that which is immoral. Nor can it command obedience to any decision serving only the human drive for dominance which can afflict even those ordained to serve. To judge a pope or a bishop, to call him to account for failing to fulfill his ministry, is in the nature of the case perilous. It can be hazardous for the individual, for if he judges unfairly or precipitously, he endangers his own commitment to the Church. It can be dangerous for the Church, for it could undermine the respect due those consecrated to be the shepherds of men. (In no case, of course, do we have the right to judge the conscience of another, only his actions.)

Yet to fail to render judgment when it is needed can be no less perilous. There is a piety in the Church which would deny this last assertion. It would hold that, for the sake of discipline and good order, one should remain silent about the faults of those in authority. This is a piety which confuses the Church with an army, believing that above all else nothing must occur which would jeopardize the efficiency of the command structure. But the existence of the Church does not depend upon its ability to maintain a temporal allegiance and discipline. Its existence depends on the Holy Spirit, and Christ has promised that, in the Spirit, He would remain with the Church. Yves Congar has pointed to a forgotten passage: " 'On those who have a right faith, the Holy Spirit bestows the perfect grace of knowing how those who are at the head of the Church must teach and safeguard all things' " —adding that this "was not written by some slavophil upholder of *sobornost,* but by St. Hippolytus. . . ." [7] A refusal to pass judgment implies that authority is not part of the

[7] *Lay People in the Church* (London: Geoffrey Chapman, 1959), p. 272.

Church: not subject to the same God as other members of the Church, nor to the duties and responsibilities which are those of all Christians, nor to the requirements of humility and responsiveness to the Holy Spirit demanded of every Catholic. It would make of those who rule a law unto themselves, not servants of the servants of God but their sovereign lords; only Christ is the Lord.

There does not exist in the Church a system of checks and balances of the kind one finds in constitutional democracies. Though at the present time the Church urgently needs some formal means of ensuring the rights of individuals, such means would remain, finally, limited. For authority in the Church has been empowered by Christ to teach in His name, and to command obedience in His name. Nonetheless, it is a part of the Church. If the Church does not remind authority of its obligations, then who will? If the individual who sees abuses, failures, omissions, opportunities endangered, does not speak to authority, then who will? There are many conceivable ways in which the Holy Spirit can influence the Church. One of the most natural would be by working through the people. But this will not be possible if the people shut their eyes, if a false piety, or a desire to preserve the self-confidence of authority seals their lips.

Honest Doubt

"What is at stake in the 'search for honesty,'" John Cogley has written, "is a larger, more total commitment to truth than the mere avoidance of lies. It is a desire to be a whole person, in public as well as in private; it is a desire to face up squarely to *all* that one believes to be true and to acknowledge candidly that the acceptance of so many truths and different kinds of truths as are open to modern man can be, and frequently is, the source of tensions." [8] For my part, as I have indicated in earlier chapters, one of the most important sources of tension is an awareness that the self one grows up with is in great part the product of social conditioning, much of it beyond the individual's control. This is as true of the religious self as it is of the self as a socialized being in society. The perception of this conditioning can be a moment of sudden awakening, or it may come in a more gradual way. In any case, it is a perception which should force one to take steps to get at the root of one's faith, both faith in God and faith in the Church.

Unhappily, at the very outset the Catholic will face a threatening obstacle if he believes it to be a moral fault to have a doubt, as some theologians have claimed; for it would then seem to him that a full exploration of his faith would be unacceptably dangerous. He is faced with an impossible choice: if he is to be honest with himself he must admit any doubts; but if he has doubts he sins against faith. The dilemma could hardly be worse. Is there here any honorable way out?

Again, we are faced with a false, but common, dilemma. Any man who, knowing God, deliberately turns himself from God will of necessity be a sinner. Such a man is culpably guilty. But what of the case of one whose faith slips away from him, either because he finds himself unable to believe any longer on philosophical grounds or because he finds that the object of faith, God, no longer has any meaning for him? It is the fear of these possibilities, a fear often instilled by the full weight of instruction and admonition, which can paralyze the Catholic who would examine his faith in depth.

[8] "Honesty vs. Loyalty Oaths," *The Commonweal,* LXXX (May 22, 1964), 250.

This was a problem skirted by the First Vatican Council in the "Constitution on Faith." In Chapter 3 of that Constitution the Fathers declared that "the most gracious God strengthens by His grace those whom He has brought out of darkness into His wonderful light so that they may persevere in this same light, and does not desert anyone unless He is first deserted. . . . those who have received the faith from the teaching authority of the Church may never have a just cause [justam causam] to alter or to doubt their faith." The minimal purpose of this declaration, it is widely agreed, was to exclude the possibility that a Catholic could have *objective* grounds [justam causam] on which to deny or suspend his faith.

This definition is, of course, not a surprising position: the Church can hardly grant the possibility that reason could discover grounds sufficient to reject the revelation of Christ and the authority granted the Church by Him. Yet to affirm this does not exhaust the problem; the question which is likely to be of greatest concern to a person intent on advancing in honesty is whether a real doubt or a loss of faith is *ipso facto* a sin, regardless of the subjective state of the doubter. While a few theologians have argued such a position, a substantial number of theologians have concluded that the point was not defined by Vatican I. That Council, in brief, did not formally exclude the possibility that a Catholic could *believe* that he had apparently rational grounds for departing from the faith or from the teaching of the Church, and "it did not pronounce on the culpability in individual cases." [9]

[9] Roger Aubert, *Le Problème de L'Acte de Foi* (2nd ed.; Louvain: Louvain University Publications, 1950), p. 219. For a different approach see G. Van Noort, *Dogmatic Theology*, Vol. III, *Divine Faith*, trans. J. J. Castelot and W. H. Murphy (Westminster, Md.: Newman Press, 1961), pp. 323 ff.

That these cases would be exceptional does not change the situation. An important implication here is that no individual whose faith is troubled need feel himself obliged to deny himself an examination of that faith on the grounds that he would necessarily sin should that examination prove destructive of his faith. As in all other instances concerning culpable guilt the decisive criterion will be the rectitude of one's conscience.

To fear a loss of faith is reasonable, but it is unreasonable to violate one's conscience to give it false support. Father Eric D'Arcy has put the matter succinctly in an analysis of the thought of Thomas Aquinas: "It has been held that it is sinful to act against a misguided conscience. If it is now held that it is sinful also to follow it, then a man sins whatever he does—an insupportable view." [10] For most theologians this dilemma has been resolved by an affirmation of two principles: "First, the supreme authority of conscience is recognized, not only in the negative sense that one is forbidden to act against it, but also in the positive sense that one is obliged to follow it; provided, of course, that one's conscience is formed in good faith. . . . Second, it is recognized that an action is formally good if it is done in accordance with conscience. This is true whether the judgment of conscience is objectively correct or erroneous; the only condition is that it has been reached in good faith." [11] Thus it is possible to conclude that no Catholic need evade a close, critical examination of his faith; in the end, his right to follow his conscience, even if the Church may judge that conscience to be objectively erroneous, has been upheld by the Church itself.

[10] *Conscience and Its Right to Freedom* (New York: Sheed & Ward, 1962), p. 111.
[11] *Ibid.,* pp. 121, 124.

Let me confess here that I find it somewhat distasteful to be forced to point to theological analyses of the kinds just cited; one might wish the rights of conscience were accepted as self-evident. I do so because, however well established, the Church's principles on the rights of the conscience remain an obscure terrain for many Catholics, perhaps now seen well enough when it is a matter of the non-Catholic conscience, but still taken to be extremely hazardous when applied in their own case. Unless a Catholic is fully clear on his rights of conscience, however, he is likely to be bedeviled by a massive onslaught of confusion, fear, and uncertainty when critical problems arise. It is hardly any wonder that a crisis of faith for a Catholic will normally be accompanied by acute anxiety; and this anxiety will be all the stronger if he has been taught to believe that the fault for having a crisis must lie solely with himself.

It may at this point seem somewhat strange to lay a special emphasis on the extreme case of basic doubts about the faith itself, whether these doubts concern the substance of revelation or the divinely inspired teachings of the Church. But it is precisely because such doubts raise the problem of personal freedom so starkly that they are worthy of examination. If, even there, a Catholic has ground on which to stand in seeking to probe the depths of his selfhood (as I believe he does), he will be in a far better position to experience a liberating sense of freedom in coping with the less critical problems that he will encounter as a Catholic. There will still remain the necessity of taking the trouble, and generating the courage, to look deeply into the self, but at least one important obstacle will have been removed. It is perfectly possible for doubt to spring from a moral failure of one kind or another; yet there is no reason to assume a priori that this is so. A thorough probing of the self will raise this as a possibility—along with many other possibilities, no one of which need be accorded initially a greater weight than any other.

In the concrete realities of the spiritual life, however, it may be relatively rare for crises of faith to present themselves in a tidy fashion. Cardinal Newman wrote that "doubt itself is a positive state, and implies a definite habit of mind, and thereby necessarily involves a system of principles and doctrines all its own." [12] Yet it is apparent that a crisis of faith may arise where these conditions for genuine doubt do not exist; indeed, one might say that for purposes of self-examination, a genuine doubt would be easier to cope with than an array of obscure difficulties intermingled with elements of doubt. A Catholic who came to believe, for example, that the Church's teaching on the resurrection of Christ was simply false, would at least know where he stood; and would presumably know what critical reasons led him to that conclusion. But what of the Catholic who had no specific reason to doubt the Church's teaching but, instead, found the teaching unintelligible or personally without any meaning? Should one ask him whether he accepted the Church's teaching, he might not know what to reply. Or he might say: I am perfectly willing to assent to the Church's teaching, but I do not know what it means to assent to a doctrine which I find meaningless. The fact that the Church does not require that he understand the teaching, but only that he accept it on the testimony of the Church, may give him some meager comfort. At least he will not be willfully rebelling. Yet his problem will have been resolved only in the most formal way; concretely, he will be as much at sea as ever.

[12] James Collins (ed.), *Philosophical Readings in Cardinal Newman* (Chicago, Ill.: Henry Regnery, 1961), p. 124.

Problems of this kind must be given greater attention. My own conviction is that the contemporary Catholic is
faced with perplexities about his faith and about the Church
which shatter any simple theological apparatus that would
sharply distinguish a doubt from a difficulty. The burning
questions for the individual today are not whether this or
that doctrine can be accepted or whether the Church's authority to define dogma ought to be respected. Such questions
bear only on the magisterial rights of the Church. Instead,
the direction of Catholic self-probing today, if I interpret the
signs correctly, is toward meaning and significance. In recent
centuries, to judge at least from the concerns of older theological manuals, the apologetic credentials of Christianity pre-
occupied men's minds: Did Christ rise from the dead? Has
man been redeemed? Are the claims of the Church justified?
What must a Catholic believe in order to be saved? Similarly,
in matters of Christian ethics, men apparently wanted to
know what was a licit act and what was illicit. What is just
and what is unjust? What is a mortal sin and what is a venial
sin? These questions have by no means disappeared today,
and there is no reason to expect that they will. But they are
becoming secondary. Today men want to know what it is to
live the Christian life; what it means to be committed to
Christ and the Church; what it means to be a morally responsible person. Questions of this kind cannot be answered in
any summary fashion; even less can one reduce the answers to
tight systems, capable of being encapsulated in manuals and
textbooks. They are all questions which encompass mystery,
questions posed by the self seeking not specific directions for
this or that decision in life but some sense of what it means
for a man to engage himself with God in the first place.

It is not difficult to understand why the Catholic should

find such basic problems taking on a new urgency. Nor is it difficult to understand why the solutions of the past seem to so many to have lost their relevance. Modern man lives in a world of vast and rapid change; the social stabilities which once helped to ward off cosmic terror are disappearing; the scientific certainties which once gave man the impression that he lived in a materially unchanging world are evaporating; the belief that progress was inevitable has been dealt some shattering blows. There is no end to changes of this kind. When the Catholic today asks that the Church find a fresh language to express old insights, or a rich language for new insights, he reflects the restlessness of contemporary man and the contemporary Christian. He, too, has been cast adrift by the tide of history and human development. The Church he sees about him, even the Church engaged in renewing itself, still has about its body the garb of other eras. He does not live in those eras. They are strange and alien to him. He is thus forced, precisely because he lives only in the twentieth century, to begin all over. For some decades now, the Church has tried to avoid this renewal; fortunately, it is beginning to see that it can do so no longer. The evidence of this recognition appears on every side. It can be seen in the reluctant abandonment, in practice if not always in theory, of the attempt to merge the philosophy of St. Thomas and contemporary modes of philosophy. It can be seen in the gradual abandonment of Latin in the liturgy of the Church. It can be seen in the adoption of the techniques of form-criticism in biblical studies. It can be seen in the gradual demise of casuistry in moral theology, and with this demise the growing disinterest in the traditional language and concepts of scholastic theology.

More positive evidence, however, is to be found in the

contemporary approach to faith, best summed up in the words "encounter" and "trust." Faith, that is, finds its meaning in the meeting of the individual with God through Christ, the son of God. This meeting is characterized by trust in God, animated by an awareness of freedom and, at the same time, by a conviction that faith is a gift of God. Put differently, faith is the mode of relationship by which man engages himself with God; it is the giving of the whole self to God, confident that this giving will not be betrayed. There is nothing here to suggest that faith does not also involve an assent to certain truths about God; but the emphasis does not lie in that direction, and for a very good reason. To accept Christ is not to commit oneself to a philosophy. It is to commit oneself to a person. One must, because one remains a rational being, believe that Christ is who He says He is. The "motives of credibility"—to use a traditional phrase—do not become irrelevant. But they are now seen in a different context, one in which the motives of belief are recognized to be clearly distinguishable from the actual reality of belief. It is this latter reality which must engage the whole person.

Loss of Faith

An important consequence here is that the expression "to lose one's faith" takes on a new meaning. For if faith is a relationship with God, it is misleading to speak of faith as if it were an object of some kind; that is, as if it were a mental or emotional entity which we somehow possess within us. Understood this way, "to lose one's faith" sounds very much like the kind of loss which the expression "to lose one's car key" signifies. But there is clearly a difference if "losing one's faith" is taken to mean an inability to sustain a once living relationship with God. A person who does not "have faith" is not a person who lacks an object labeled "faith" in his mind. He is a person who does not trust God, does not know Him, is not committed to doing His will. One can further see that a loss of faith admits of degrees, just as does the possession of faith. Our trust in God can be weak or strong. "As we can grow in graces," Newman observed, "so surely can we inclusively in faith." [13] God does not fail us, but our grasp of God may wax and wane, subject to the stresses of the free mind and to the inner and outer forces which assail our consciousness. Josef Pieper, paraphrasing St. Thomas Aquinas, speaks of the "curious coexistence of certainty and uncertainty, which not only describes but actually constitutes the psychological situation of the believer." [14] There can thus be an "element of uncertainty in the act of belief. . . . it is part of the nature of belief to leave doubts possible. This possibility is based on the fact that the believer's intellect is not really satisfied; rather, the mind, insofar as it believes, is operating not on its own but on alien soil." [15]

To this last comment of Pieper's, I would add a further suggestion. In a totally Christian culture, or at least a culture dominated by Christian signs and symbols and pervaded by a Christian theology, the "alien soil" of belief may seem less strange. There will be a common language by means of which men can share and confirm each other's values. There will be a common metaphysic, even if inchoate, whereby men will share common assumptions about the nature of reality. There will be a common religious community in which men,

[13] *Ibid.*, p. 148.
[14] *Belief and Faith*, trans. Richard and Clara Winston (New York: Pantheon Books, 1963), p. 44.
[15] *Ibid.*, p. 47.

by sharing a sense of the same mystery of existence, can confirm the naturalness of their common faith. Whether such a Christian culture ever existed in all its purity is a debatable point. At any rate, the contemporary Western world no longer possesses such a culture; Christianity exists in our world, but Christendom does not. Hence, the soil of belief is more alien than ever: the traditional theological language is ceasing to convey much meaning to a generation of Catholics immersed in the very different idiom of the contemporary world; there is no common metaphysic shared by modern man—and there is ceasing to be a clear metaphysic in the Church since that once provided by Scholasticism is being replaced by a groping attempt to discern a personalist and a biblical metaphysic. There is, finally, no common religious community among men.

These are shattering changes for many, and the number of those afflicted grows as the vestiges of man's past history fade away in the face of the modern world. "The inherited 'images of the world' is the soul in which faith ripens and bears fruit, the flesh wherein the message of faith is incarnated. And when a separation is imposed, which is in a way to be expected, since the images of the world are temporary, while the message is everlasting, it is a real agony for the man who is subject to it." [16] Yet what was once perhaps an isolated agony becomes today a common one. There is terror before the cosmos, before history, before an unpredictable future. Frau Görres, in the article just cited, makes a valuable distinction between "authentic unbelief" and "blinded faith." [17] The former, she writes, "is proud of itself, and is irri-

---

[16] Ida Friederika Görres, "The Believer's Unbelief," *Cross Currents*, XI (Winter, 1961), 56.

[17] *Ibid.*, p. 57.

tated by or laughs at the spectacle of the simple believer; it confirms in their doubts those who weaken; it ridicules those who bear or represent the Church, and rejoices in their imperfections and mistakes." The latter, by contrast, "behaves quite differently. It continues walking at the modest pace of the ordinary Christian. It does not show its distress. How many among us lead this life? There are priests grappling with the intimate obscurities which devour them; nuns for whom, in the secret of their souls, everything seems to have lost all meaning. . . ." [18]

Dark Night of the Soul

Could one go so far as to say, perhaps, that it is no longer the isolated saint who will go through the "dark night of the soul" but that the whole Church, as a community, may have entered into such a night? This is a question worth considering in an age where our old concepts of God no longer seem to bring us close to Him, where Providence appears darkly veiled, where Christians find themselves more and more uncomfortable when they ask themselves why the Church seems to have so little hold upon the minds of men. Frau Görres cites a passage from the writings of a German Catholic writer, Herbert Schneider, which expressed, perhaps more than he realized, the dismay of the contemporary Christian as well as his hope: "To pray beyond faith, despite faith, despite unbelief, despite oneself, every day that a bad conscience toward the Church secretly makes its way . . . there is grace in it: there is unbelief which has its place in the realm of grace. This experience, beginning with despair before the cosmos and history, this despair before the Cross, is this to-

[18] *Ibid.*

day's Christianity? This obligation, this obscurity. . . could yet be a promise: *'numen adest,* divinity is there.' " [19]

Both anguish and hope are present in the Church today, perhaps even more than during the late fifties when Schneider wrote the words above. Despite the work of Pope John and the regenerative forces freed by the Second Vatican Council, it is not difficult to discover indications of frustration, hints of a far-reaching malaise, a bewilderment before the immensity of the problems confronting the Church. Part of this stems from a recognition that it takes a painfully long time for renewal sought at the highest levels in the Church to seep down to the lower levels. Part is due to an irrepressible feeling that the Council has barely scratched the surface of the exigencies of total renewal. Part arises from the practical resistance which many of the forms of renewal encounter among those who would hold on to the old ways. Part is due to a belief that the Council is solving problems which have already been replaced by new ones. In *Ecclesiam Suam* Pope Paul VI speaks of the "great transformations, upheavals and developments" of mankind. "All of this," he says, "like the waves of an ocean, envelops and agitates the Church." That raises the possibility, in his judgment, "that a danger bordering almost on vertiginous bewilderment can shake the Church's very foundations and lead men to most bizarre ways of thinking. . . ." But there is hope as well. There has been a Council; there is movement and there is activity. Above all, there is a perception that all is not right in the Church; however much this insight may be a source of anguish, it can also be a source of hope.

The difficult task is to keep the hope and the anguish in a proper relationship with each other. It is good for the

[19] *Ibid.,* p. 58.

Christian to hope, but this hope must have a supernatural basis and not be a naïve escapism, a grasping at straws. This means that the human experience of despair and anguish will have to be accepted. They provide the motive for an examination of faith and the Church which might otherwise be lacking. Pope Paul VI is undoubtedly right in suggesting that the present bewilderment can lead people to "most bizarre ways of thinking." But could this not indicate many possibilities not suggested by his words: that those so led are in desperate need of a nourishment they are not receiving; that men are casting about, by bold and imaginative speculations, for a new purchase on Christ and the Church; that what appears "bizarre" at the moment may turn out to be a new direction of inestimable value? Authority seems ever ready to panic when this happens—Pope Paul VI felt the need to lay a heavy stress in his encyclical on obedience—but it may be boldness which is required. There is not a serious want of obedience in the Church today; authority can have little complaint on this score. What is lacking is a conviction in the Church that the way out of the desert lies primarily in an instant response to commands. Men obey today, but they do not always know why they are obeying, nor is it always clear to them that their submission serves either their own spiritual welfare or that of the Church. To say that they do not need clarity here, but only fidelity, is a safe—and useless—observation. It is not the kind of observation which feeds man's spirit; and that feeding is what men want in their obedience. To return to Schneider: "Theology can resolve such problems, even reduce them to nothing, but without reaching the vital contents of the existential experience in which they are rooted. We can cut the mushrooms which are only protrusions, or wait for age to decompose them, but their original filament does not die. It has curled around my own roots." [20]

Faith, it is often said, entails risk. A man leaps beyond himself to touch God, to respond to the grace God offers when that grace is perceived only as the faintest glimmer in the depths of his being. Yet faith today may be said to entail still another risk: the risk of exercising one's freedom to look at one's faith. For the Catholic trained only to see faith as a precious good to be preserved, nothing may be more difficult than to take the risk of inquiring into the quality of this faith. Such an inquiry carries with it dangerous lines of exploration. It means exploring the possibility that one has been misdirected by one's parents, one's friends, one's teachers, and by the Church itself. Or that one's faith is nothing more than the product of an ecclesiastical system which, given sufficient time, would be able to make any person believe anything it might want him to. Or that one believes because one does not have the courage to break away from the securities against anxiety which faith—almost any faith—can provide. "Faith," someone once said, "is a quality of mind by which we are enabled to believe things we know to be untrue." Not every Catholic will find it easy to take this cynical definition seriously —to ask himself if even this possibility should be considered. But it must. Only a willingness to bear the pain of looking fearlessly into the self, of veering away from no possibility, will ensure that the relationship with God is a reality of the self and not the product of a will to illusion.

The same may be said, analogously, of the individual's faith in the Church. That there must be such a faith is evident. For the Catholic, faith in God and faith in the Church

[20] *Ibid.*, p. 55.

are inextricably related. It is through the Church that the Good News is brought to us. At the same time it must be kept in mind that God, realized through the Church, is the ultimate goal of our life, not the Church as a temporal institution. The Church was created by God as a means of bringing us to Him. Our earthly life in the Church is a foretaste of the community of man with man in God, but it is not that community fully realized, fully perfected. It is important to keep these distinctions clear, for there is a sense in which one could mistake an identification with the Church as a perfect identification with God. If commitment to God cannot be realized without a commitment to the Church, one must also say that a commitment to the Church must not be allowed to serve as a substitute for God. "The Church proclaims and possesses," in the words of the Lutheran sociologist Peter L. Berger, "a certain faith. This faith is addressed to each individual in his unique existence before God. He cannot hold this faith except as the unique individual he is. As a substitute for this painful acquisition of faith, the individual can instead identify with the Church, the social collectivity which . . . holds that faith as an ideology. His real act of decision, then, is not toward the Church that claims to possess it. By identifying with the Church he deludes himself into thinking that he has made a decision of faith." [21]

The only way in which one can ensure that his own faith in the Church is not just the acceptance of an ideological identity masquerading as a genuine relationship with God through the community of the Church is, again, by asking himself hard questions about that faith. He must discern whether his acceptance of the Church rests on a fear of breaking with

[21] *The Precarious Vision* (Garden City, N.Y.: Doubleday and Co., 1961), pp. 180–181.

his family and friends, whether it stems from a desire to have a
social identification, whether it represents merely a fear of
thinking and deciding for himself, whether he perhaps sees
it as having a utilitarian value for society and thus worthy
of support. There is, of course, the possibility that all
of these motives may coexist with a genuine faith; but that,
too, is worth knowing, for to the extent that they do they en-
danger the purity of faith, debasing it by unworthy motives
and inclinations. When large numbers of Catholics are so inclined, the Church as a whole will inevitably be affected. The
people of God will then be shading off into a collectivity of
discrete individuals, each using the Church to work out his
own psychological and sociological difficulties. A Church
which is seen by its members as a special form of group ther-
apy will become a Church in name only.

Faith and Responsibility

This ever present danger makes the honesty of the individual about his own faith in God and in the Church crucial for the life of the whole Church. A person who is not
determined to be responsible for the integrity of his own
faith will hardly have a lively conviction of his responsibility
for the Christian community. By the same token, one who
has sought to purify his own inner life will be in a better
position to discern the misdirections and the failures of the
community. One reason, perhaps, why local churches have
failed to speak prophetically to men of social evils—one
thinks here of the Church in the American South, the
Church in Germany during the Nazi period, the Church in
Italy and in Latin America, socially dormant for so long—is
that the members of those churches saw the Church too much

in terms of an individualistic way to personal salvation, or as a bulwark of social stability, or as an element of national self-identification. Whatever accusations may justly be directed at episcopal leadership for sustaining these ills, they alone can hardly be held responsible for the failure of a whole people. Leadership was needed, but needed as well were Catholics who had radically interrogated themselves and who were, as a result, sufficiently strong in their own resources to withstand the pressures of custom, inertia, nationalism, and the desire for psychological security.

For the sake of the Church, then, a person must be an individual to the very roots of his being. His responsibility to himself will animate the community of all men. He can show the Church what it is to respond to the dictates of conscience; what it is fearlessly to dare to ask dangerous questions; what it is to establish a self which is one's own; what it is to refuse to accept conformity as a way of life. A person who does not dare to interrogate the Church, to interrogate his own deepest convictions, will not be equipped to interrogate society. A Church made up of men and women who do not know the demands of honesty within the Church cannot be expected to resist the dishonesties of society. A Christian who cannot enter into an honest relationship with himself will find it difficult to enter into an honest relationship with others. A Church which does not encourage and provide the conditions necessary for honesty cannot expect to gain the perception of itself required to fulfill its mission. A Catholic who does not seek honesty with himself has no grounds for expecting the Church to be honest with him. Dishonesty is a disease which generates its own life: pretense calls forth pretense, evasions encourage evasions, falsehoods create other falsehoods. The Church must teach men how to be honest. Men must teach the Church.

Date Due